Pay Off Your Mortgage Early *With Excel!*

Create an
Optimal Payoff Plan
for Your Income

Tim Hill

Questing Vole Press

Pay Off Your Mortgage Early With Excel! Create an Optimal Payoff Plan for Your Income
by Tim Hill

Copyright © 2020 by Questing Vole Press. All rights reserved.

Editor: Kevin Debenjak
Proofreader: Diane Yee
Compositor: Kim Frees
Cover: Questing Vole Press

Contents

1 **Getting Started with Loans & Mortgages**.......... 1
   Downloading the Sample Workbook............................. 2
   Using the Example Formulas 2
   The Time Value of Money... 4
   Timing Issues... 4
   Cash Flows 5
   The Basic Financial Functions 6
   Rounding Numbers 9
   Rounding Examples...10

2 **Present Value (PV)**..13
   Picking an Interest Rate 13
   Present Value of an Annuity 14
   Present Value of a Lump Sum 15
   Present Value of an Annuity with a Lump Sum 16
   Deferred-Start Payments..17
   Variable Payments..17

3 **Future Value (FV)** 19
   Future Value of Payments... 20
   Future Value of a Lump Sum...21
   Future Value of Payments and a Lump Sum................. 22

4 **Payments (PMT)** 23
   Loan Payments 24
   Retirement Payments 24

5 Interest Rates (RATE) 25
Short-Term Loans 26
Growth Rates 26
Interest-Free Loans 27

6 Periods (NPER) 29
Years Until Retirement 30
Early Loan Payoff 31
Credit Card Payoff 32

7 Interest and Principal Components 33
Single Payments (IPMT and PPMT) 33
Cumulative Payments (CUMIPMT and CUMPRINC) 35

8 Converting Interest Rates 37
Types of Quotes 37
Conversion Formulas (EFFECT and NOMINAL) 38

9 Loan Amortization Schedules 41
Uniform Payment Schedules 42
Flexible Payment Schedules 44

10 Summarizing Loan Options 49
One-Way Data Tables 50
Two-Way Data Tables 52

11 Getting Started with Dates & Times 55
Downloading the Sample Workbook 55
Using the Example Formulas 56
Entering and Formatting Dates and Times Quickly 57

12 Date & Time Basics 59
Date Serial Numbers 59
Entering Dates 60
Time Serial Numbers 63
Entering Times 65
Combining Dates and Times 66
Formatting Dates and Times 67
Problem Dates 68

13 Date & Time Functions 71
TODAY and NOW: Inserting the Current Date and Time 71
DATE and TIME: Inserting Any Date or Time 72
DAY, MONTH, and YEAR: Extracting Part of a Date 75
SECOND, MINUTE, and HOUR: Extracting Part of a Time 76
DATEVALUE and TIMEVALUE: Converting Text to a Date or Time 77
WEEKDAY: Determining the Day of the Week 78
DAYS360: Counting Days Between Two Accounting Dates....... 78
EDATE: Adding and Subtracting Months 79
YEARFRAC: Calculating the Fraction of a Year Between Two Dates 80
EOMONTH: Finding the Last Day of a Month 81
NETWORKDAYS: Counting Business Days 82
WORKDAY: Offsetting a Date by a Number of Business Days . 82
WEEKNUM: Calculating the Week Number of a Year 83
DATEDIF: Calculating the Difference Between Dates 83

14 Date Tricks 85
Basic Date Arithmetic 85
Generating a Series of Dates 86
Converting Text to Dates 88
Converting a Year to Roman Numerals 88
Calculating a Person's Age 89
Determining Whether a Year is a Leap Year 89
Determining the Number of Days Remaining in a Year 90
Determining the Ordinal Day of a Year 90
Determining Which Quarter a Date Falls In 90
Determining the Previous Weekday 91
Determining the Next Weekday 91
Determining the Nth Occurrence of a Weekday in a Month 92
Counting Occurrences of a Weekday in a Month 93
Calculating Easter Sunday 93

15 Time Tricks 95
Basic Time Arithmetic 95
Generating a Series of Times 97

Converting Text to Times 98
Rounding Times 99

16 Getting Started with Sums & Counts 101
Downloading the Sample Workbook 102
Using the Example Formulas 102
Sums and Counts without Formulas 104

17 Counting Basics 107
Counting Functions 107
Basic Counting Formulas 108

18 Counting Tricks 113
Counting Cells Based on a Single Criterion (COUNTIF) 113
Counting Cells Based on Multiple Criteria (COUNTIFS) 115
Counting the Most Frequently Occurring Value (Mode) 119
Counting Unique Values 121
Counting Text Strings 122

19 Frequency Distributions 125
Using the FREQUENCY Function 125
Using Custom Formulas 128
Using the Analysis ToolPak 129
Using a Pivot Table 132

20 Summing Basics 133
Summing Functions 133
Basic Summing Formulas 134
Using AutoSum 136

21 Summing Tricks 139
Calculating a Cumulative Sum 139
Summing Extreme Values 141
Summing Currency Amounts 142
Summing Every Nth Value in a Range 143
Summing Values Based on a Single Criterion (SUMIF) 144
Summing Values Based on Multiple Criteria (SUMIFS) 147

Index 151

1   Getting Started with Loans & Mortgages

Calculations with mortgages, student loans, leases, credit-card debt, car payments, medical expenses, annuities, and retirement funds are the most common financial operations in Excel. Part I (Chapters 1–10) of this book shows you how to use worksheet functions, data tables, and other Excel features to manage your business and personal finances. If you're using an older version of Excel that doesn't support the latest worksheet functions, then you'll find equivalent formulas that work in Excel 2003 or earlier.

- Learn about basic financial concepts, including cash flows, timing issues, and the time value of money.

- Calculate the present value to determine how much to invest now to meet a future goal.

- Compute the future value to see how money will accumulate in your retirement or savings accounts.

- Figure out the payments needed to pay off a loan or to meet an investment target.

- Derive the true interest rate of your investments or loans, including "interest-free" loans.

- See how much time it will take to pay off a loan, meet an investment target, or retire.

- Separate the interest and principal portions of your mortgage or loan payments for tax purposes.
- Convert between the commonly used methods of quoting interest rates.
- Create amortization schedules to see how your debts change over time.
- Build summary tables to compare loans that have different interest rates, loan amounts, or payment terms.
- Master the auxiliary skills needed to create financial workbooks: Dates & Times (Chapters 11–15) and Sums & Counts (Chapters 16–21).

Downloading the Sample Workbook

To follow along with or copy the examples in this book, download the Excel workbook excel_loans_mortgages.xlsx from *questingvolepress.com* (a .xls workbook is also included for pre-2007 versions of Excel). This workbook contains worksheets that demonstrate most the example formulas. The following figure shows a worksheet from the sample workbook.

Tip: If you're using Excel 2007 or later and sharing your workbooks with people using earlier versions of Excel, then read the Microsoft support article, "Save an Excel workbook for compatibility with earlier versions of Excel" at *support.office.com*.

Using the Example Formulas

When you adapt the example formulas in this book to use in your own Excel workbooks, keep the following issues in mind.

Named Ranges

Some of the example formulas use **named ranges** as function arguments: COUNT(data) or SUM(values), for example. When you use these formulas in your own worksheets, substitute either the actual

[Screenshot of an Excel spreadsheet showing a loan amortization table with columns for Date, Interest rate, Payment, Additional Principal, Interest, Principal, and Balance.]

range reference (A1:E8, for example) or a range name defined in your workbook (Formulas tab > Defined Names group > Name Manager).

If your data are in a table, then you can use table referencing in your formulas instead of creating named ranges. For example, if a table named Table1 has a column named Payment, then you can enter

```
=COUNTIFS(Table1[Payment],">=500",
Table1[Payment],"<=1000")
```

instead of manually creating a range named Payment and entering

```
=COUNTIFS(Payment,">-500",Payment,"<=1000")
```

When you define a range as a table (Insert tab > Tables group > Table), Excel creates names automatically for the table and for each column in the table.

Array Formulas

A formula that's surrounded by braces { } is an **array formula**. For example,

```
{=SUM(IF(ISTEXT(values),1))}
```

Whenever you enter an array formula, you must press Ctrl+Shift+Enter (not just Enter). Don't type the braces manually; they will appear automatically in the formula bar. If you edit an existing array formula,

Chapter 1   Getting Started with Loans & Mortgages   3

then you must still press Ctrl+Shift+Enter; otherwise, the array formula will revert to a normal formula and return the wrong result. For details, read the Microsoft support article "Guidelines and examples of array formulas" at *support.office.com*.

Circular References

A formula that refers back to its own cell, either directly or indirectly, is a **circular reference**. If the formula =COUNT(A1:C3), for example, is entered in any cell in the range A1:C3, then Excel opens the Circular Reference Warning message box. Circular references are sometimes useful (notably in some financial and scientific calculations) and Excel can solve them iteratively, but they're most often unintentional. For details, read the Microsoft support article "Remove or allow a circular reference" at *support.office.com*.

The Time Value of Money

The concept of **time value of money**, or **TVM**, means that the value of money varies over time. If you're given the choice of receiving $1000 now or $1000 in a year, for example, then you'd take the cash now because:

- You can invest the $1000 now. If you earn a positive return, then the sum of the $1000 and interest earned will be worth more than the future $1000.

- You might never see the future $1000 if the payer goes bankrupt, or reneges, or dies, or whatever.

The time value of money is the central concept in finance. It's why banks charge you interest on loans, and pay you interest on deposits; it's why sellers give a discount when you pay early (or pay cash); and it's why lotteries pay out less when you take the lump-sum option. This book shows you how to use Excel to calculate the value of money in the past, present, or future.

Timing Issues

Timing is crucial in financial transactions. Consider the following timing and calendar issues in your formulas.

Time Periods of Interest Rates

The time period that your payment covers must match the time period of your interest rate. If you plug a *monthly* payment into a financial function, along with an *annual* interest rate, then the result will be wrong. To fix the formula, convert the interest rate to a monthly rate so that it matches the payment frequency. When you see an interest rate divided by 12 in a formula, it usually means that an annual interest rate is being converted to a monthly interest rate.

Date of First Payment

In most transactions, the first payment is made after the first month (or whatever period payments are normally made). If you get a loan on June 1, for example, then you probably don't have to make the first payment until July 1. In some financial transactions, however, the first payment is made right away. In Excel's financial functions, you specify the timing of the first payment by using the *type* argument. If the first payment is made **in arrears** (at the end of the first period), then set *type* to 0 (zero) or omit this argument. If the first payment is made **in advance** (at the beginning of the first period), then set *type* to 1.

Tip: Down payments aren't regular payments, so they don't affect which *type* value to specify.

Days vs. Nights

In common usage, financial transactions refer to the number of *days* between two dates. It's actually clearer and more accurate to refer to the number of *nights*, since that's what's actually being counted. Night-counting is what banks use to calculate interest. If you deposit money and then withdraw it the next day, for example, then the bank pays you interest for only one night, not two days. If you deposit and then later withdraw money on the same day, then you earn no interest (zero nights).

Cash Flows

All financial formulas involve **cash flows**. Cash that's flowing out is a **payment** and cash that's flowing in is a **receipt**. When you create a financial formula, think in terms of cash flows. In Excel's financial functions, positive cash flows (flowing in) are shown as positive values, and negative cash flows (flowing out) are shown as negative values. Because you use the same functions whether you're calculating investments or loans, you must use positive or negative numbers in your formulas. The rules of thumb are:

- If it's money that's coming *to* you, whether you're receiving a loan or an investment that's matured, then the number is positive.

- If it's money that's leaving your hands, whether it's a deposit *to* an account or a payment *for* a loan, then the number is negative.

Two examples:

- **You take out a mortgage to buy a house.** When you borrow the money for the house, it's a positive cash flow. Future mortgage payments are negative cash flows.

- **You buy a car on credit.** The bank gives you cash to buy a car (positive cash flow to you). In the future, you will pay back that money (negative cash flow to you).

The signs of the cash flows always reflect *your* perspective. In the examples above, the *bank's* cash flows have the same amounts but opposite signs.

Using incorrect signs is one of the most common errors in financial formulas. You can often spot these errors by looking for obviously incorrect results. If you decrease the amount of money borrowed and the monthly payment increases, for example, then one of your numbers probably has the wrong sign. If the returned value is unusually large or small, or is growing or shrinking too slowly or rapidly, then try modifying the formula by changing the numbers or flipping their signs, and watch how the result changes. Using incorrect signs can also cause a function to return a #NUM! error.

The Basic Financial Functions

Excel's five basic financial functions—PV, FV, PMT, RATE, and NPER—are covered in detail in later chapters. The syntax of these functions, with optional arguments in [brackets], is:

PV(*rate, nper, pmt, [fv], [type]*)
Returns the present value of an investment.

FV(*rate, nper, pmt, [pv], [type]*)
Returns the future value of an investment.

PMT(*rate, nper, pv, [fv], [type]*)
Returns the periodic payment for an annuity.

RATE(*nper, pmt, pv, [fv], [type], [guess]*)
Returns the interest rate per period of an annuity.

NPER(*rate, pmt, pv, [fv], [type]*)
Returns the number of periods for an investment.

These financial functions are related because they deal with different aspects of the same transaction, so many of the arguments are the same from function to function. The common arguments and their meanings are:

- **rate.** The interest rate, expressed as a percentage, that's paid on a loan or used to discount future cash flows. The period that the interest rate covers must be the same period used for *nper* and *pmt*. You can think of this value as the rate at which an investment or loan will increase or decrease over time. If an investment has an annual interest rate of five percent, then after one year the future value will be five percent larger than the present value.

Tip: To enter a percentage in Excel, type either the fractional number (0.0525, for example) or use the % operator (5.25%). For a refresher on entering and formatting percentages in Excel, read the Microsoft support article "How to do percentages in Excel" at *microsoft.com*.

- **nper.** The total number of payment periods between the present value and the future value of an investment or loan. This value can be the number of payments on a loan, for example, or the number of periods that money is kept in a bank account. The number of periods must be expressed in the same terms as *rate* and *pmt*. A

30-year mortgage with monthly payments, for example, has an *nper* of 360 (30 × 12). If an investment distributes interest quarterly and you invest your money over a two-year period, then *nper* is 8 (4 × 2).

- **pmt**. The amount of each payment (money that you contribute to an investment or loan). For these financial functions, the payments must be the same amount and made at regular intervals. The payment amount is normally made up of both principal and interest.

- **fv**. The **future value**, or the value of an investment or loan at some point in the future. This value is the final cash flow that settles the transaction. In many cases, the payments settle the transaction (pay off the loan, for example), so a future value doesn't exist.

- **pv**. The **present value**, or the value of an investment or loan at the very beginning of its life. This value is the first cash flow that starts the transaction, such as borrowing money (the principal) on a loan or depositing money (the initial balance) into a bank account. If the transaction is made up of only payments, then a present value might not exist.

- **type**. Determines whether the payments are made in arrears (0 or omitted) or in advance (1).

- **guess**. An initial approximation of the expected result. When calculating an interest rate, Excel iterates to converge on an answer. If you provide a guess that's close to the actual result, then Excel can iterate faster. If you omit *guess*, then Excel uses 0.1 (10%). Excel usually converges if *guess* is between 0 and 1.

You can plug in different values for the arguments to, say, compare deals, prepare a counteroffer, or explore the sensitivity of a transaction. Excel's Goal Seek feature is particularly useful for finding the value of an argument that returns the desired result. In Excel 2007 or later, choose Data tab > Data Tools group > What-If Analysis > Goal Seek. In Excel 2003 or earlier, choose Tools > Goal Seek.

This book also covers the related functions IPMT, PPMT, CUMIPMT, CUMPRINC, EFFECT, and NOMINAL. Excel actually has dozens more financial functions, but they're typically used by bond traders, accountants, and professional investors.

Tip: In Excel 2010, Microsoft improved the accuracy of PMT and some other financial functions. If you're using Excel 2007 or earlier, then some of your results might differ slightly from those shown in this book. For details, read the Microsoft support article "What's New: Changes made to Excel functions" at *support.office.com*.

Rounding Numbers

When working with financial formulas, you're going to have to devote some thought to **rounding**, the process by which you adjust fractional numbers so that they're less precise but more tractable or in standard form. Financial pros (and statisticians) know that there are many ways to round numbers, and that they all have their own problems. Excel offers many rounding functions, but the most useful ones for financial calculations are ROUND, ROUNDUP, and ROUNDDOWN.

Tip: Other rounding functions, which are useful in some situations, include MROUND, CEILING, FLOOR, INT, TRUNC, EVEN, ODD, DOLLARDE, DOLLARFR, ISO.CEILING (Excel 2010 or later), CEILING.MATH (Excel 2013 or later), and FLOOR.MATH (Excel 2013 or later).

Many types of financial calculations can lead to rounding errors when summing a large group of values. Even "off-by-a-cent" values can accumulate to large errors when many such values are totaled. To prevent cumulative errors, round only the final calculated value. Don't round intermediate results.

Excel's rounding functions all use a technique called **arithmetic rounding**, which always rounds the number 5 up, and can cause rounding biases. Consider the number 1.5, for example, which lies exactly halfway between the numbers 1 and 2. In arithmetic rounding, 1.5 is always rounded up to 2. This convention can bias your results if you're rounding many numbers and then summing them (because the five digits 5, 6, 7, 8, and 9 are always rounded up, versus the four digits 1, 2, 3, and 4, which are always rounded down).

The best option for avoiding rounding biases is to calculate first, and round later. Never sum numbers that you've already rounded. Alternatively, you can use **banker's rounding**, which rounds 5 up sometimes and down other times, depending on whether it's paired with an even or odd number. For example, 1.5 is rounded up to 2, but 2.5 is rounded down to 2, 3.5 is rounded up to 4, and so on. This technique lets you sum a long column of rounded numbers without biasing the result.

Excel doesn't provide a built-in function that does banker's rounding, but Microsoft provides custom VBA (Visual Basic for Applications) macros that do so. For details, read the Microsoft support article "How To Implement Custom Rounding Procedures" included with the sample workbook download.

Keep in mind that the actual values in cells can have additional decimal places that are hidden by the number format. The value 14.0772, for example, appears as $14.08 if the cell is formatted as a currency amount with two decimal places. To quickly apply the Currency format with two decimal places (negative numbers in parentheses), press Ctrl+Shift+$. To apply the General number format (all decimal places visible), press Ctrl+Shift+~. (For a list of keyboard shortcuts, read the Microsoft support article "Keyboard shortcuts in Excel" at *support.office.com*.)

Rounding Examples

The ROUND function rounds a given number (the first argument) to the specified number of digits (the second argument). The following formula, for example, returns 145.68 (145.6789 rounded to two decimal places):

```
=ROUND(145.6789,2)
```

To round a number to the nearest integer, set the second argument of ROUND to zero. The following formula returns 146:

```
=ROUND(145.6789,0)
```

If the second argument of ROUND is negative, then the number is rounded to the left of the decimal point. The following formula, for example, returns 150:

```
=ROUND(145.6789,-1)
```

Because ROUND uses arithmetic rounding, numbers ending in 5 are rounded *away* from zero (either up or down). The following formula, for example, returns 11:

```
=ROUND(10.5,0)
```

The next formula returns −11 (rounding away from zero):

```
=ROUND(-10.5,0)
```

To force rounding in a particular direction, use the ROUNDUP or ROUNDDOWN function. The following formula, for example, returns 10 (rounding down to the nearest whole number).

```
=ROUNDDOWN(10.5,0)
```

The next formula returns 145.85:

```
=ROUNDDOWN(145.8599,2)
```

The following formula returns 11 (rounding up to the nearest whole number):

```
=ROUNDUP(10.2,0)
```

The next formula returns 145.23:

```
=ROUNDUP(145.2222,2)
```

When rounding a currency value to two decimal places (that is, to the nearest cent), you can round up to the nearest cent, round down to the nearest cent, or round to the nearest cent (which can round up or down).

To round up to the nearest 0.01 (one cent), use the CEILING function. The following formula rounds the value in cell A1 up to the nearest cent:

```
=CEILING(A1,0.01)
```

To round down to the nearest cent, use the FLOOR function:

```
=FLOOR(A1,0.01)
```

To round to the nearest cent, use the ROUND function:

```
=ROUND(A1,2)
```

You can also round to specific multiples. To round up to, say, the nearest five cents, type:

```
=CEILING(A1,0.05)
```

To round down to the nearest five cents, type:

```
=FLOOR(A1,0.05)
```

To round to the nearest five cents, use the MROUND function:

```
=MROUND(A1,0.05)
```

Tip: In Excel 2003 or earlier, you must load the Analysis ToolPak add-in to use the MROUND function. To do so, choose Tools menu > Add-Ins > select Analysis ToolPak > OK.

---

2 Present Value (PV)

The PV function returns the present value of future cash flows, telling you how much that future money is worth now. The syntax of PV, with optional arguments in [brackets], is:

PV(*rate, nper, pmt,* [*fv*], [*type*])

The real use of PV is to answer hypothetical questions. If you know what interest rate you can get for your money, how long you'll be invested, and what future value you hope to attain, then PV can answer the question: What initial amount of money must I come up with now? For example, the formula:

=PV(6%/12,10*12,0,100000)

answers the question: To end up with $100,000 how much money must I invest initially, assuming a 6% annual interest rate (compounded monthly) and a maturation period of ten years (10 × 12 months)? The PV function returns –$54,963.27. The negative result indicates that you must pay out this money at the beginning.

Picking an Interest Rate

Often the tough part about using the PV function is picking an interest rate (the *rate* argument), and the one that you choose depends on your personality. Are you optimistic? Pessimistic? Conservative? Immoderate? Some people use the historical rate of stock-market returns, whereas others use the rate that they would get on an unsecured bank loan. Still others use the interest rate on a risk-free investment, such as a U.S. Treasury note. You'll find no shortage of advice if you go looking for it.

Present Value of an Annuity

You can use the PV function to calculate the present value of a series of future receipts, called an **annuity**. If you receive one payment of $1000 each year for five years, for example, then the value now of those payments assuming a 6% annual interest rate is:

=PV(6%,5,1000,0,0)

	A	B	C
1		PV Annuity	PV Annu
2	Rate:	6.00%	
3	Periods:	5	
4	Payment:	$1,000.00	
5	Future value:	$0.00	
6	Type:	0	
7			
8	Present value:	($4,212.36)	

(B8, fx =PV(B2,B3,B4,B5,B6))

The result is −$4212.36. In other words, if the payer offered you more than $4212.36 right now (instead of making periodic payments to you in the future), then you would take it. If the payer offered you less, then you would refuse and wait for the regular payments.

The interest rate of 6% in this example means that you can invest the $4212.36 now to earn a 6% annual return, and end up in the same financial position as if you had just waited for the $1000 payments.

If the situation is reversed so that you're the payer rather than the payee, then the formula uses a negative cash flow:

=PV(6%,5,-1000,0,0)

The result, $4212.36, also has the opposite sign of the preceding result.

In both examples, the total of all payments makes up the entire transaction, so the future value is zero. The default value of the optional *fv* and *type* arguments is zero, but they're included here for clarity.

C8		f_x =PV(C2,C3,C4,C5,C6)	
	A	C	D
1		PV Annuity	PV Lump
2	Rate:	6.00%	
3	Periods:	5	
4	Payment:	($1,000.00)	
5	Future value:	$0.00	
6	Type:	0	
7			
8	Present value:	$4,212.36	

Present Value of a Lump Sum

You can also use the PV function if the payment is just a single large future cash flow—a **lump sum**—rather than a periodic annuity. If you're going to be paid $1000 five years from now, then the value now of that future amount is:

=PV(6%,5,0,1000)

D8		f_x =PV(D2,D3,D4,D5,D6)	
	A	D	E
1		PV Lump Sum	PV Annuity + L
2	Rate:	6.00%	
3	Periods:	5	
4	Payment:	0	
5	Future value:	$1,000.00	
6	Type:	0	
7			
8	Present value:	($747.26)	

The result is −$747.26. The payment is a cash inflow (a positive $1000) that will occur five years from now. This result means that if you had $747.26 now and invested it to earn 6% annually, then it would be worth $1000 in five years. Because there are no payments, the *type* argument is irrelevant.

Present Value of an Annuity with a Lump Sum

The PV function can calculate the present value of an annuity coupled with a lump-sum payment. If you're going to be paid $1000 per month for five years and then also be paid $10,000 at the end of the five years, then the value now of all your future cash inflows is:

=PV(6%/12,5*12,1000,10000,0)

	A	E
		PV
1		Annuity + Lump Sum
2	Rate:	6.00%
3	Periods:	5
4	Payment:	$1,000.00
5	Future value:	$10,000.00
6	Type:	0
7		
8	Present value:	($59,139.28)

(E8 formula: =PV(E2/12,E3*12,E4,E5,E6))

The result is −$59,139.28. Because the $1000 payments are made monthly, the *rate* and *nper* arguments must be converted to months: *rate* is divided by 12 (for 12 months) and *nper* is 5 × 12 (for 60 months; not 5 for five years).

If the first payment is made now (in advance) rather than a month from now (in arrears), then the formula is:

=PV(6%/12,5*12,1000,10000,1)

and the result is −$59,397.91.

Deferred-Start Payments

You can calculate the present value of a regular series of cash flows with a deferred start by nesting PV functions. Suppose that you can afford loan repayments of $1000 per month, and your deal with the bank lets you defer the first payment for 12 months. If the bank quotes a 6% rate on a ten-year loan, then the amount that you can borrow is:

=PV(6%/12,12,0,-PV(6%/12,10*12,-1000))

	A	B	C	D
11		PV Deferred-Start Payments		
12	Rate:	6.00%		
13	Periods:	10		
14	Payment (1):	($1,000.00)		
15	Deferral period:	1		
16	Payment (2):	$0.00		
17				
18	Present value:	$84,840.67		

B18 ▾ f_x =PV(B12/12,B15*12,B16,-PV(B12/12,B13*12,B14))

The result is $84,840.67. To understand how this formula works, break it into steps. First, calculate the present value of the payments, which is $90,073.45 (the result of the inner PV function). This value is used as the future value argument of the outer PV function. The outer PV function further discounts this amount over the year deferral period, and results in $84,840.67. In other words, if you borrow $84,840.67 now, then this amount will increase to $90,073.45 in one year with no payments, and it will decrease to zero in ten years with $1000 monthly payments.

Variable Payments

You can calculate the present value when the payments change over time by chaining and nesting PV functions. Suppose that you hold a nine-year lease with the following payment schedule:

- Years 1–3: $1000/month
- Years 4–6: $2000/month
- Years 7–9: $3000/month

For a 6% interest rate, the present value of the lease is:

```
=PV(6%/12,3*12,-1000)+
PV(6%/12,3*12,0,-PV(6%/12,3*12,-2000))+
PV(6%/12,6*12,0,-PV(6%/12,3*12,-3000))
```

	A	B	C	D	E	F
		B27	fx =PV(B22/12,3*12,B23)+PV(B22/12,3*12,0,-PV(B22/12,3*12,B24))+PV(B22/12,6*12,0,-PV(B22/12,3*12,B25))			
21		PV Variable Payments				
22	Rate:	6.00%				
23	Payment (1-3):	($1,000.00)				
24	Payment (4-6):	($2,000.00)				
25	Payment (7-9):	($3,000.00)				
26						
27	Present value:	$156,669.74				

The result is $156,669.74. To understand how this formula works, break it into three steps:

- Years 1–3: Calculate the present value of the first three years of $1000 payments normally.

- Years 4–6: Calculate the second three years by using the deferred-start technique. The present value of its $2000 payments are calculated, and that value becomes the future value argument to a different PV function. That future value is discounted over a three-year deferred period (while the $1000 payments are being made in years 1–3).

- Years 7–9: The last three years of $3000 payments are discounted similarly but over a six-year deferral period (while the $1000 and $2000 payments are being made in years 1–3 and years 4–6).

3 Future Value (FV)

The FV function calculates the future value of an investment, assuming a fixed interest rate. FV lets you factor in regular payments, so you can calculate how money accumulates in a retirement or savings account. The syntax of FV, with optional arguments in [brackets], is:

FV(*rate, nper, pmt,* [*pv*], [*type*])

To understand how FV works, suppose that you invest $1000 at a fixed interest rate of 5% annually. At the end of the year, this investment's going to be worth $1050.00:

=1000*105%

This calculation returns the future value—that is, the initial 100 percent of the principal that you invested plus an additional five percent in interest income.

If you reinvest the five percent interest payment for an additional year, then you end up with $1102.50:

=1000*105%*105%

Simple calculations like these require no help from Excel's financial functions, but real transactions usually aren't so simple. Two common problems that are messy to solve by using the type of formula shown above are:

- You deposit money in a savings account that pays interest monthly. Even though the annual interest rate is the same as in the examples above, your money accumulates faster, thanks to **compound interest** (that is, interest earned on the interest you previously earned).

- You make regular deposits to an investment account. You can't calculate this extra amount of money separately because it also accumulates interest, starting from the date on which you deposit it.

For these and similar transactions, using the FV function is the alternative to constructing complex and inflexible formulas.

To rewrite the formula above to calculate the return on a $1000 investment after one year of earning 5% annual interest, type:

=FV(5%,1,0,-1000,0)

The result is $1050.00.

If you reinvest the five percent interest payment for an additional year, then you end up with $1102.50:

=FV(5%,2,0,-1000,0)

Note the signs (directions) of the cash flows in the preceding FV formulas. From your perspective, the payment (*pmt*) is zero and the initial balance (*pv*) is negative. Even though money is accumulating for you, the initial balance and the regular payments represent money you're handing over (outflows), so these numbers must be zero or negative. The final value is positive because that's the total you get back.

Future Value of Payments

Starting next month, you deposit $100 monthly in a new savings account that earns 2% annual interest. In 20 years, the account will have $29,479.68:

=FV(2%/12,20*12,-100,0,0)

The 2% annual percentage rate is converted into a monthly rate, and the 20 years is converted into months. There's no present value because you just opened the account, and *type* is 0 (zero) because you're starting next month (in arrears).

	B8	▼	f_x =FV(B2/12,B3*12,B4,B5,B6)

	A	B	C
1		FV Payments	FV Lump Sum
2	Rate:	2.00%	
3	Periods:	20	
4	Payment:	($100.00)	
5	Present value:	$0.00	($50,0
6	Type:	0	
7			
8	Future value:	$29,479.68	$162,1

Future Value of a Lump Sum

You deposit $50,000 in a new retirement account earning 4% and make no other deposits or withdrawals. In 30 years, you'll have $162,169.88:

=FV(4%,30,0,-50000,0)

The -$50,000 is money that's flowing away from you and into the retirement account. The result, $162,169.88, is money that's flowing from the account to you.

	C8	▼	f_x =FV(C2,C3,C4,C5,C6)

	A	C	D
1		FV Lump Sum	F Payments +
2	Rate:	4.00%	
3	Periods:	30	
4	Payment:	0	
5	Present value:	($50,000.00)	
6	Type:	0	
7			
8	Future value:	$162,169.88	

Future Value of Payments and a Lump Sum

You can use FV to calculate the future value when there's an initial amount and you plan to add to or subtract from that amount regularly.

You make monthly payments of $1043.29 against your $200,000 mortgage. The mortgage interest rate is 4.75%. In five years, you will still owe $182,996.79 on your house:

```
=FV(4.75%/12,5*12,-1043.29,200000,0)
```

D8		f_x =FV(D2/12,D3*12,D4,D5,D6)	
	A	D	E
1		FV Payments + Lump Sum	
2	Rate:	4.75%	
3	Periods:	5	
4	Payment:	($1,043.29)	
5	Present value:	$200,000.00	
6	Type:	0	
7			
8	Future value:	($182,996.79)	
9			

The payments are monthly, so *rate* and *nper* are converted to months: the annual interest rate is divided by 12, and the number of years is multiplied by 12. The current balance (*pv*) of the mortgage is a cash inflow (positive number) even though no cash is actually flowing in. This cash inflow actually occurred when you first bought the house: the bank paid you $200,000 in exchange for a promise to repay it, and you in turn used the money to buy the house from its previous owner. (This formula covers the period from now until five years from now, so it doesn't involve the time when the original funds actually flowed in to you.)

4 Payments (PMT)

The PMT function calculates the amount of regular payments that you must make either to pay off a loan or to meet an investment target. You specify the present value and future value of the loan or investment and the rate of interest over its lifetime, and PMT returns the payment that you must make in each time period. The syntax of PMT, with optional arguments in [brackets], is:

PMT(*rate, nper, pv,* [*fv*], [*type*])

If you don't specify a future value (*fv*), then PMT assumes that it's 0 (which is correct if you want to see how long it'll take to pay off a loan). The *type* argument indicates whether you make the first payment at the end of the payment period (0 or omitted) or at the beginning (1).

Loan Payments

You buy a $35,000 car by making a down payment of $5000 and financing the rest with a three-year 1.8% dealer loan. Your monthly payments are $856.66:

```
=PMT(1.8%/12,3*12,30000,0,0)
```

	A	B	C
1		PMT Loan Payments	PMT Retirement Paymer
2	Rate:	1.80%	4
3	Periods:	3	
4	Present value:	$30,000.00	($800,00
5	Future value:	$0.00	$100,00
6	Type:	0	
7			
8	Payment:	($856.66)	$4,57

B8 ▼ f_x =PMT(B2/12,B3*12,B4,B5,B6)

Retirement Payments

You retire with $800,000 in your retirement account. To withdraw monthly payments to live on for the next 20 years and still have a $100,000 safety net left over at the end of the twentieth year, you can take out $4575.20 every month, assuming a 4% annual return:

```
=PMT(4%/12,20*12,-800000,100000,0)
```

	A	C	D
1		PMT Retirement Payments	
2	Rate:	4.00%	
3	Periods:	20	
4	Present value:	($800,000.00)	
5	Future value:	$100,000.00	
6	Type:	0	
7			
8	Payment:	$4,575.20	

C8 ▼ f_x =PMT(C2/12,C3*12,C4,C5,C6)

5 Interest Rates (RATE)

The RATE function determines the interest rate that's needed to achieve a certain future value, given an initial balance, and a fixed amount for regular contributions. The syntax of RATE, with optional arguments in [brackets], is:

RATE(*nper, pmt, pv,* [*fv*], [*type*], [*guess*])

Because there's no direct way ("closed-form solution") to determine the desired interest rate for multiple-payment transactions, the math underlying the RATE function is more complex than that used in the other financial functions. RATE uses an **iterative** (trial and error) approach to converge on an answer. In most cases, RATE returns an answer quickly, but if it can't converge within 20 iterations, then RATE fails and returns a #NUM! error.

You can specify an optional *guess* argument, which tells RATE which interest rate to try first. If you omit a guess, then RATE assumes 10 percent initially, and works from there. Use an appropriate time scale for the guess (if you make monthly payments, divide the annual interest rate by 12). The number returned by RATE uses the same time scale.

Use realistic numbers with RATE or you might try to calculate the impossible. If you try to find the interest rate needed to pay off a $10,000 two-year loan by making $400 monthly payments, for example, then RATE returns a negative value (meaning there's no way to meet the goal unless the bank pays *you* interest). A little arithmetic reveals that the total amount of monthly payments ($400 × 24) is only $9600—not even enough to pay off the $10,000 principal, let alone the interest.

Short-Term Loans

Small, short-term unsecured loans, called **payday loans**, are usually paid back in 14 days (when the borrower's next paycheck comes in) and are characterized by excessive rates of interest. If you borrow $200 and agree to pay $240 in 14 days, then the annual interest rate is 521.43%:

=RATE(1,0,200,-240,0,0.01)*365/14

The period (*nper*) is one because the loan has only one payment. The period of one actually represents a 14-day period, so the rate is converted to an annual percentage rate by dividing by 14 days and multiplying by 365 days. The result, 521.43%, is so large because the term is so short.

B9		fx	=RATE(B2,B3,B4,B5,B6,B7)*365/14
	A	B	C
1		RATE Short-Term Loans	RATE Growth Rates
2	Periods:	1	24
3	Payment:	$0.00	($200.00)
4	Present value:	$200.00	($50,000.00)
5	Future value:	($240.00)	$56,000.00
6	Type:	0	0
7	Guess:	1%	1%
8			
9	Rate:	521.43%	2.27%

Tip: Interest rates are often stated as annual percentage rates (APRs), even if the term of the loan is more or less than a year. Converting rates to APR, regardless of the term, lets you compare different loans. For details, see Chapter 8.

Growth Rates

You have $50,000 in your retirement account at the beginning of the year. You deposit $200 per twice-monthly paycheck in the account all year (24 payments), and have $56,000 at the end of the year. The annual growth rate is 2.27%:

=RATE(24,-200,-50000,56000,0,0.01)*24

RATE returns the growth rate over each of the 24 periods, so you must multiply the result by 24 to get the annual growth rate of 2.27%.

C9   *fx* =RATE(C2,C3,C4,C5,C6,C7)*C2

	A	C	D
1		RATE Growth Rates	RATE Interest-Free Loans
2	Periods:	24	
3	Payment:	($200.00)	($2,000)
4	Present value:	($50,000.00)	$1,500
5	Future value:	$56,000.00	$0
6	Type:	0	
7	Guess:	1%	
8			
9	Rate:	2.27%	56.

Interest-Free Loans

You buy a $2000 TV and pay for it in 12 monthly "interest-free" payments. You later find out that you could have paid $1750 cash to buy the same TV. The seller actually built the interest into the purchase price, so you effectively paid $250 in interest on a $1750 one-year loan, or 25.40%:

=RATE(12,-2000/12,1750,0,0,0.01)*12

D9   *fx* =RATE(D2,D3/D2,D4,D5,D6,D7)*D2

	A	D	E
1		RATE Interest-Free Loans	
2	Periods:	12	
3	Payment:	($2,000.00)	
4	Present value:	$1,750.00	
5	Future value:	$0.00	
6	Type:	0	
7	Guess:	1%	
8			
9	Rate:	25.40%	

6 Periods (NPER)

The NPER function calculates the amount of time it will take you to pay off a loan or meet an investment target, provided you already know the initial balance, the interest rate, and the amount you're prepared to contribute to each payment. The syntax of NPER, with optional arguments in [brackets], is:

NPER(*rate, pmt, pv,* [*fv*], [*type*])

Tip: If NPER returns a fractional result (12.34 months, for example), then you can round up to the nearest integer time period for the final payment. For details, see "Rounding Numbers" on page 9.

Years Until Retirement

You need $700,000 to retire, and you're contributing $200 per month. The current balance of your retirement account is $400,000. If you can earn 4% on your investments, then you can retire in 150.9 months (12.6 years):

```
=NPER(4%/12,-200,-400000,700000,0)
```

	A	B	C
1		NPER Years Until Retirement	
2	Rate:	4.00%	
3	Payment:	($200.00)	
4	Present value:	($400,000.00)	
5	Future value:	$700,000.00	
6	Type:	0	
7			
8	Periods (months):	150.9	

Fixed Weekly Income

If you know how much you need to live on each week, then you can combine NPER and PV. Continuing from the preceding example, if you can live on $1000 per week, you can retire in 157.0 months (13.1 years):

```
=NPER(4%/12,-200,-400000,PV(4%/52,20*52,-1000,0,0),0)
```

	A	B	C	D	E
11		NPER Fixed Weekly Income			
12	Rate:	4.00%			
13	Payment:	($200.00)			
14	Present value:	($400,000.00)			
15	Periods (PV):	20			
16	Fixed payment (PV):	($1,000.00)			
17	Future value (PV):	$0.00			
18	Type:	0			
19					
20	Periods (months):	157.0			

The PV function in the *fv* argument of NPER assumes that you'll earn 4% (converted to weeks), that you'll withdraw money for 20 years (converted to weeks), that you'll withdraw $1000 per week, and that there will be nothing left at the end of the twentieth year.

Early Loan Payoff

Interest rates are falling, and you decide to refinance your home mortgage. You have a $250,000 mortgage balance at 5.0%, with monthly payments of $1649.89 for the next 20 years. If you refinance to 3.75% but retain the same payment, then you can shave 34.4 months (2.9 years) off the loan:

```
=(20*12)-NPER(3.75%/12,PMT(5.0%/12,20*12,250000,0,0),
250000,0,0)
```

B32   ƒx =(B27*12)-NPER(B25/12,PMT(B26/12,B27*12,B28,B29,B30),B28,B29,B30)

	A	B	C	D	E	F
24		NPER Early Loan Payoff				
25	Rate (new):	3.75%				
26	Rate (old):	5.00%				
27	Periods (years):	20				
28	Present value:	$250,000.00				
29	Future value:	$0.00				
30	Type:	0				
31						
32	Periods (months):	34.4				

The *pmt* argument of NPER is a PMT function that calculates the $1649.89 that you're paying based on the terms of your existing mortgage (alternatively, you can plug in a mortgage payment directly instead of using PMT). Subtracting the result from 240 (20 years of 12 months) shows how many months that your mortgage is reduced by when you refinance.

Credit Card Payoff

Your outstanding credit card balance is $10,000 at 18%. You cut up the card and pay down the debt at $200 per month. You'll be debt-free in 93.1 months (7.8 years):

```
=NPER(18%/12,-200,10000,0,0)
```

	B42	▼	ƒx	=NPER(B36/12,B37,B38,B39,B40)	
	A		B		C
35			**NPER** **Credit Card Payoff**		
36	Rate:		18.00%		
37	Payment:		($200.00)		
38	Present value:		$10,000.00		
39	Future value:		$0.00		
40	Type:		0		
41					
42	Periods (months):		93.1		

7 Interest and Principal Components

For tax purposes or other reasons, you might need to know how much of a particular payment or series of payments constitutes interest, and how much goes toward paying down the debt (the principal).

Single Payments (IPMT and PPMT)

The PPMT and IPMT functions both analyze a single loan payment. PPMT calculates the amount of a payment that goes toward paying off the loan's principal, while IPMT calculates the amount of a payment that pays back accrued interest.

Tip: If you've created an amortization schedule (Chapter 9), then these functions aren't particularly useful because you can simply refer to the schedule.

PPMT and IPMT take the same arguments as the PMT function with one difference: you must specify the period of the loan or investment. This argument, *per*, tells the function which payment to analyze. A *per* of 1, for example, examines the first payment. A *per* of 12 analyzes the twelfth payment, which, assuming you pay back the loan on a monthly basis, occurs at the end of your first year of repayment. The syntax of IPMT and PPMT, with optional arguments in [brackets], is:

    IPMT(rate, per, nper, pv, [fv], [type])
    PPMT(rate, per, nper, pv, [fv], [type])

As with all amortization functions, the *rate, per,* and *nper* arguments must match in terms of the time period. If the loan term is measured in months, then *rate* must be the interest rate per month, and *per* must be a particular month. Set *per* ≤ *nper*, or the function will return a #NUM! error.

Over the course of a loan, the amount you pay toward your principal will gradually increase, and the amount going to pay interest will decrease. But for each payment, it's always true that PMT = PPMT + IPMT. In other words, your total monthly payment remains the same until you pay off the loan.

For a 30-year $100,000 mortgage at 6% interest, for example, the interest and principal portions of the first payment are:

```
=IPMT(6%/12,1,30*12,100000)
=PPMT(6%/12,1,30*12,100000)
```

The results are –$500.00 interest and –$99.55 principal. The portion of a payment that pays down the debt is smaller at the beginning of the loan because the interest portion is higher (because of the higher balance). It's jarring to see how little of the first payment goes toward actually paying down the debt.

	A	B	C	D	E
1	Rate:	6.00%			
2	Years:	30			
3	Present value:	$100,000.00			
4	Future value:	$0.00			
5	Type:	0			
6					
7					
8	Payment number:	1	12	180	360
9	IPMT:	($500.00)	($494.39)	($356.46)	($2.98)
10	PPMT:	($99.55)	($105.16)	($243.09)	($596.57)
11	Sum:	($599.55)	($599.55)	($599.55)	($599.55)
12					
13	PMT:	($599.55)	($599.55)	($599.55)	($599.55)

B9 f_x =IPMT(B1/12,B8,B2*12,B3,B4,B5)

The interest and principal portions of the final (360th) payment are:

```
=IPMT(6%/12,360,30*12,100000)
=PPMT(6%/12,360,30*12,100000)
```

The results are −$2.98 interest and −$596.57 principal. The formulas for the other payments are the same except that the *per* argument reflects the payment being calculated.

Cumulative Payments (CUMIPMT and CUMPRINC)

The IPMT and PPMT functions show the interest and principal components for a single payment. The CUMIPMT and CUMPRINC functions show the same components but for a specified series of payments. The syntax of CUMIPMT and CUMPRINC (all arguments are required) is:

CUMIPMT(*rate, nper, pv, start_period, end_period, type*)
CUMPRINC(*rate, nper, pv, start_period, end_period, type*)

For a 30-year $100,000 mortgage at 6% interest, for example, the cumulative interest and principal portions of the first 12 payments are:

=CUMIPMT(6%/12,30*12,100000,1,12,0)
=CUMPRINC(6%/12,30*12,100000,1,12,0)

The results are −$5966.59 interest and −$1228.01 principal. The formulas for the other series of payments are the same except that the *start_period* and *end_period* arguments reflect the range of payments being calculated.

Tip: You can get the same information by creating an amortization schedule (Chapter 9).

	B9		f_x	=CUMIPMT(B1/12,B2*12,B3,B7,B8,B4)		
	A	B		C	D	E
1	Rate:	6.00%				
2	Years:	30				
3	Present value:	$100,000.00				
4	Type:	0				
5						
6						
7	Start payment:	1		13	181	1
8	End payment:	12		24	360	360
9	CUMIPMT:	($5,966.59)		($5,890.85)	($36,870.25)	($115,838.19)
10	CUMPRINC:	($1,228.01)		($1,303.75)	($71,048.84)	($100,000.00)
11	Sum:	($7,194.61)		($7,194.61)	($107,919.09)	($215,838.19)

Chapter 7 Interest and Principal Components 35

8 Converting Interest Rates

The interest rate transforms a present value into a future value. Or, when operating as a discount rate, transforms a future value into a present value. This chapter describes terms and techniques for working with interest rates in financial formulas.

Types of Quotes

If you put $1000 in an investment that pays an interest rate of 10 percent per year, then you'll have $1100 at the end of the first year: the original $1000 investment plus $100 in earned interest. At the end of the second year, you would earn an additional $110 in interest (10 percent of $1100). Adding interest earned to an investment is called **compounding**, and the total interest earned (the normal interest plus the extra interest on the reinvested interest—the extra $10, in this example) is called **compound interest**.

Interest can also be compounded within the year. Suppose that your $1000 investment earns 10 percent compounded semiannually. At the end of the first six months, you receive $50 in interest (five percent of the original $1000 investment). This $50 is reinvested, and for the second half of the year, you earn five percent of $1050, or $52.50. Therefore, the total interest earned in the first year is $102.50. In other words, the interest rate appears to actually be 10.25 percent.

Understanding which interest rate to use (here, 10 percent or 10.25 percent) means knowing how interest rates are commonly quoted:

- **Nominal rate.** The nominal rate is the annual rate before compounding (here, the 10 percent rate). The nominal rate is always quoted along with the compounding frequency (here, 10 percent compounded semiannually). The nominal annual interest rate is often called the **annual percentage rate**, or **APR**.

- **Effective rate.** The effective rate is the annual rate that an investment actually earns in the year after the compounding is applied (here, the 10.25 percent rate).

Most banks and lenders quote nominal rates compounded monthly. When comparing interest rates or reporting investment returns, however, effective rates are more commonly quoted to make it easier to compare rates.

Tip: Another type of quote, called the **periodic rate** is simply the nominal rate divided by the compounding period. A 6% APR compounded monthly is a periodic rate of 0.5% per month (6%/12), for example.

Conversion Formulas (EFFECT and NOMINAL)

To convert between nominal and effective rates, use the EFFECT and NOMINAL functions:

```
EFFECT(nominal_rate, npery)
NOMINAL(effect_rate, npery)
```

nominal_rate is the nominal annual interest rate, *effect_rate* is the effective annual interest rate, and *npery* is the number of compounding periods per year.

The formula to convert a nominal rate of 10% compounded semiannually to an effective rate is:

```
=EFFECT(10%,2)
```

The result is 0.1025, or 10.25% (as calculated manually in the example above). This rate is the actual interest that's paid or earned in a year. The formula to convert a nominal rate of 10% compounded monthly to an effective rate is:

```
=EFFECT(10%,12)
```

The result is 10.4713%.

	D3		f_x	=EFFECT(C3,B3)	
	A	B		C	D
1	Compounding frequency	Compounding periods		Nominal rate	Effective rate
2	Annually	1		10.00%	10.00%
3	Semiannually	2		10.00%	10.25%
4	Quarterly	4		10.00%	10.38%
5	Monthly	12		10.00%	10.47%
6	Weekly	52		10.00%	10.51%
7	Daily	365		10.00%	10.52%

If you paid $61.68 in interest last year on a $1000 loan, then your nominal interest rate was 6.0% APR compounded monthly:

=NOMINAL(61.68/1000,12)

A 10% effective rate converted to a nominal rate compounded semiannually is 9.76%:

=NOMINAL(10%,2)

	D12		f_x	=NOMINAL(C12,B12)	
	A	B		C	D
10	Compounding frequency	Compounding periods		Effective rate	Nominal rate
11	Annually	1		10.00%	10.00%
12	Semiannually	2		10.00%	9.76%
13	Quarterly	4		10.00%	9.65%
14	Monthly	12		10.00%	9.57%
15	Weekly	52		10.00%	9.54%
16	Daily	365		10.00%	9.53%

9 Loan Amortization Schedules

An **amortization schedule** is a table detailing each periodic payment on an amortizing loan (typically a mortgage). **Amortization** is the process of paying off a debt over time through regular payments. A portion of each payment is for interest while the remaining amount is applied to paying down the principal balance.

Over the course of a loan, the part of each payment that's applied to principal varies (with the remainder going to interest), and an amortization schedule shows the specific amounts put toward interest and principal for each payment. The portion of a payment that pays down the debt is smaller at the beginning of the loan because the interest portion is higher (because of the higher balance).

Uniform Payment Schedules

The following figure shows a simple amortization schedule for a 30-year $100,000 mortgage at a fixed annual rate of 4.5%. Rows 15 through 363 are hidden, so that only the first six and final six months of payment activity are visible. This schedule is inflexible because it doesn't support variable interest rates, additional principal payments, and other dynamic loan features, but it serves as a precursor for the flexible amortization schedule in the next section.

	A	B	C	D	E	F
	payment		fx =ROUND(PMT(interest_rate/12,term*12,-loan_amount),2)			
1	Loan amount:	$100,000.00				
2	Annual interest rate:	4.50%				
3	Term (years):	30				
4	Loan date:	15-Jun-2013				
5	Payment amount:	$506.69				
6						
7	Date	Payment	Interest	Principal	Balance	
8	Totals	$182,408.40	$82,404.57	$100,003.83		
9	15-Jun-2013				$100,000.00	
10	15-Jul-2013	$506.69	$375.00	$131.69	$99,868.31	
11	15-Aug-2013	$506.69	$374.51	$132.18	$99,736.13	
12	15-Sep-2013	$506.69	$374.01	$132.68	$99,603.45	
13	15-Oct-2013	$506.69	$373.51	$133.18	$99,470.27	
14	15-Nov-2013	$506.69	$373.01	$133.68	$99,336.59	
364	15-Jan-2043	$506.69	$11.24	$495.45	$2,501.44	
365	15-Feb-2043	$506.69	$9.38	$497.31	$2,004.13	
366	15-Mar-2043	$506.69	$7.52	$499.17	$1,504.96	
367	15-Apr-2043	$506.69	$5.64	$501.05	$1,003.91	
368	15-May-2043	$506.69	$3.76	$502.93	$500.98	
369	15-Jun-2043	$506.69	$1.88	$504.81	($3.83)	

The blue-shaded cells B1:B4 are the user-input area. You can enter the loan amount, interest rate, term (in years), and loan date. The formula in cell B5 is:

```
B5: =ROUND(PMT(interest_rate/12,term*12,
     -loan_amount),2)
```

The PMT function calculates the monthly payment amount based on the inputs (for details, see Chapter 4). Because the payments are made monthly, the interest rate (B2) is divided by 12 and the term (B3) is multiplied by 12 to convert them to a monthly basis. Loan payments aren't paid in fractions of cents, so the ROUND function rounds the result of PMT to the nearest cent (two decimal places); for details, see "Rounding Numbers" on page 9.

Row 7 shows descriptive labels. Row 8 shows total payments, interest, and principal:

```
B8: =SUM(B9:B369)
C8: =SUM(C9:C369)
D8: =SUM(D9:D369)
```

These totals can be placed at the bottom of the schedule as well, but putting them at the top reduces scrolling.

The amortization schedule itself starts in row 9, with the loan's start date (cell B4, named loan_date) and beginning balance (cell B1, named loan_amount):

```
A9: =loan_date
E9: =loan_amount
```

Payments start in row 10, a month after the loan's start date. The formula in cell A10 uses the DATE function to increment the preceding date by one month:

```
A10: =DATE(YEAR(A9),MONTH(A9)+1,DAY(A9))
```

(An alternative formula is =EDATE(A9,1).)

Cell B10 simply refers to the monthly payment (calculated by PMT in cell B5):

```
B10: =payment
```

Cell C10 calculates the monthly interest based on the previous balance (in cell E9) and rounds the result to the nearest cent:

```
C10: =ROUND(E9*interest_rate/12,2)
```

Cell D10 calculates the portion of the monthly payment that goes toward reducing the principal balance by subtracting the interest portion from the entire payment:

```
D10: =B10-C10
```

Cell E10 updates the balance by subtracting the principal portion of the monthly payment:

```
E10: =E9-D10
```

To complete the amortization schedule, the five formulas in row 10 are copied down to the end of the table (to row 369). The final balance at the end of the term is zero (or close to zero, given rounding errors).

Flexible Payment Schedules

Building on the preceding example, the following figure shows an enhanced amortization table that lets you change the term, interest rates, and payments. Making these changes usually causes the loan's maturity date to change, but this schedule handles updates automatically, with no need to insert or delete rows of formulas. The middle rows are hidden so you can see the last payment.

	payment		fx	=ROUND(PMT(interest_rate/12,term*12,-loan_amount),2)			
	A	B	C	D	E	F	G
1	Loan amount:	$100,000.00					
2	Annual interest rate:	4.50%					
3	Term (years):	30					
4	Loan date:	15-Jun-2013		9			
5	Payment amount:	$506.69					
6							
7	Date	Interest rate	Payment	Additional Principal	Interest	Principal	Balance
8	Totals		$204,538.50	$1,000.00	$105,538.50	$100,000.00	
9	15-Jun-2013						$100,000.00
10	15-Jul-2013	4.50%	$506.69		$369.86	$136.83	$99,863.17
11	15-Aug-2013	4.50%	$506.69		$381.67	$125.02	$99,738.15
12	20-Sep-2013	4.50%	$506.69		$442.67	$64.02	$99,674.13
13	15-Oct-2013	4.50%	$506.69		$307.21	$199.48	$99,474.65
14	15-Nov-2013	5.00%	$506.69		$422.43	$84.26	$99,390.39
15	15-Dec-2013	5.00%	$506.69		$408.45	$98.24	$99,292.15
16	15-Jan-2014	5.00%	$506.69	$1,000.00	$421.65	$1,085.04	$98,207.11
17	15-Feb-2014	5.00%	$506.69		$417.04	$89.65	$98,117.46
18	15-Mar-2014	5.00%	$506.69		$376.34	$130.35	$97,987.11
405	15-Jun-2046	5.00%	$506.69		$18.29	$488.40	$3,819.38
406	15-Jul-2046	5.00%	$506.69		$15.70	$490.99	$3,328.39
407	15-Aug-2046	5.00%	$506.69		$14.13	$492.56	$2,835.83
408	15-Sep-2046	5.00%	$506.69		$12.04	$494.65	$2,341.18
409	15-Oct-2046	5.00%	$506.69		$9.62	$497.07	$1,844.11
410	15-Nov-2046	5.00%	$506.69		$7.83	$498.86	$1,345.25
411	15-Dec-2046	5.00%	$506.69		$5.53	$501.16	$844.09
412	15-Jan-2047	5.00%	$506.69		$3.58	$503.11	$340.98
413	15-Feb-2047	5.00%	$342.43		$1.45	$340.98	$0.00
414							

The user-input area (cells B1:B4) and payment calculation (cell B5) are the same as in the uniform payment schedule, but you should no longer think of these values as applying to the entire life of the loan.

Row 7 shows descriptive labels. Row 8 shows total payments, additional principal, interest, and principal. The formula in cell C8 is:

C8: =SUMIF($G10:$G490,">=0",C10:C490)

This formula sums only the relevant rows, accounting for the dynamic maturity date, which can shorten or lengthen depending on the inputs. This SUMIF function sums only those payments in column C up to the point where the balance in column G falls to zero (that is, where the loan is completely amortized). This formula is copied across to the additional principal, interest, and principal columns (anchored in each case to column G by the absolute column reference):

```
D8:  =SUMIF($G10:$G490,">=0",D10:D490)
E8:  =SUMIF($G10:$G490,">=0",E10:E490)
F8:  =SUMIF($G10:$G490,">=0",F10:F490)
```

The amortization schedule itself occupies the range A9:G490. You can change the blue-shaded cells. This schedule's formulas account for changes that in some cases affect only one payment, and in other cases affect a payment *and* all subsequent payments.

Row 9 holds the loan's start date (B4) and beginning balance (B1):

```
A9:  =loan_date
G9:  =loan_amount
```

Changing Payment Dates

Changing a payment date in a shaded cell in column A affects only that one payment. If you make one late payment, for example, then it doesn't mean that all subsequent payments will be late. In this example, the third payment (row 12) was made five days late on 20-Sep-2013, having no effect on the remaining payments, which were all made on time. The formula in cell A10 is:

```
A10: =DATE(YEAR(loan_date),MONTH(loan_date)+ROW()-
ROW(first_payment)+1,DAY(loan_date))
```

This formula increments the month from the fixed loan date (cell B4, named loan_date), not from date of the payment before it. Because the payments start in row 10, the current row number minus 9 is used to increment the month (cell G9 is named first_payment). This formula is copied down to all the rows. You can overwrite any shaded date formula in column A with a literal date value. The change will affect the interest and principal calculations but not the rest of the dates.

Changing Interest Rates

If you change an interest rate in a shaded cell in column B, then it changes for all subsequent payments (until it changes again or the loan matures). The formula in cell B10 references the initial interest rate in cell B2 (named interest_rate):

```
B10:  =interest_rate
```

The rest of the cells in column B refer to the values directly above them. The formula in cell B11:

```
B11:  =B10
```

repeats the previous month's rate, and is copied down to all the rows. If you enter a new interest rate, then that rate continues down the schedule until you change it again manually. In this example, the bank raised the rate to 5% for the fifth payment (row 14) and all subsequent payments.

Calculating Payments and Paying Additional Principal

The payment in column C doesn't change unless the remaining balance is less than the normal payment, then only the balance (plus interest) is paid. To pay additional principal along with a normal payment, enter the extra amount in a blue-shaded cell in column D. In this example, an additional $1000 is applied to the seventh payment (row 16). The formula in cell C10:

```
C10:  =IF(G9+E10<payment+D10,G9+E10-D10,payment)
```

is copied down to all the rows.

Calculating Interest

The interest calculation in column E accounts for early or late payments (that is, changes to the payment dates in column A). Instead of dividing the interest rate by 12, the rate is multiplied by a ratio of the number of days outstanding to 365. The formula in cell E10:

```
E10:  =ROUND(G9*B10*(A10-A9)/365,2)
```

is copied down to all the rows. The ROUND function rounds the result to the nearest cent.

Calculating Principal

The principal calculation in column F accounts for any additional principal payments in column D. The formula in F10:

```
F10: =C10+D10-E10
```

is copied down to all the rows.

Calculating Balance

The balance in column G is calculated subtracting the principal portion of the current payment from the previous balance. The formula in G10:

```
G10: =G9-F10
```

is copied down to all the rows.

Applying Conditional Formatting

In the figure above, you can see that the final payment occurs in row 413. The schedule's formulas actually continue down to row 490, but conditional formatting, starting in row 10, hides all results after the balance becomes zero or negative. If the value in column G of the row above is zero or less, then both the background (fill) color and the font color are white, rendering them invisible.

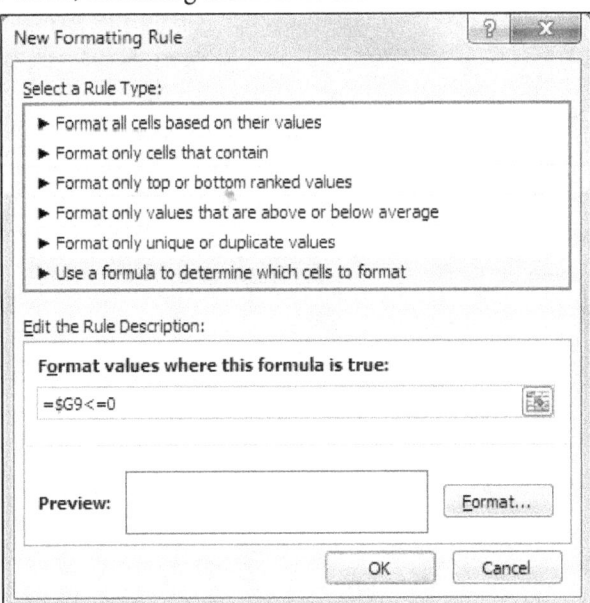

To apply conditional formatting, select the range A10:G490 and then choose Home tab > Styles group > Conditional Formatting > New Rule. Select the rule type "Use a formula to determine which cells to format" and then add the rule description:

```
=$G9<=0
```

The absolute column ($G) makes every column in the selection refer to column G; the relative row (9) makes every row refer to the row above it. Click Format, choose a white font color and a white fill color, and then click OK. Click OK again to apply the conditional formatting to the selection.

In this example, the formulas continue past row 413, but conditional formatting hides them in rows 414 through 490 (the end of the table).

10 Summarizing Loan Options

Excel's Data Table feature can help you easily compare loans that have different interest rates, loan amounts, or payment terms. A **data table** is a dynamic range that summarizes formula cells for varying input cells (limited to one or two input variables at a time).

Tip: If data tables slow workbook calculation, then choose Formulas tab > Calculation group > Calculation Options > Automatic Except for Data Tables. (In Excel 2003 or earlier, choose Tools menu > Options > Calculation tab.) Then, to recalculate a data table manually, select its formulas and then press the F9 key. For details, read the Microsoft support article "Calculate multiple results by using a data table" at *support.office.com*.

One-Way Data Tables

A **one-way data table** shows the results of any number of calculations for different values of a single input cell. The following figure shows the layout of a one-way data table.

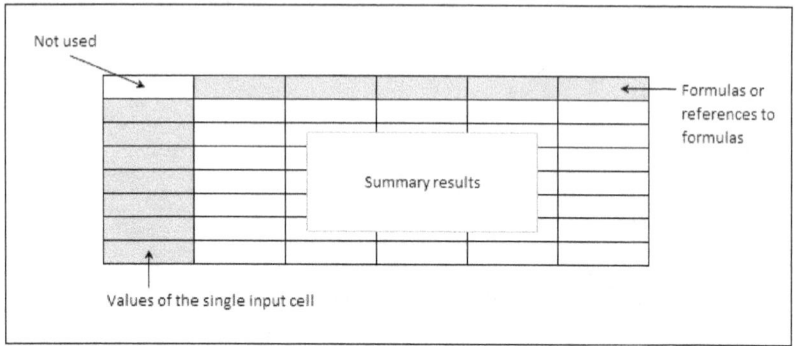

The following figure shows a one-way data table (in D2:G10) that displays three calculations (payment amount, total payments, and total interest) for a 30-year $100,000 mortgage, using nine different interest rates ranging from 4.5% to 6.5%. The input cell is B2. (The cells E1:G1 are descriptive labels and aren't part of the data table.)

	A	B	C	D	E	F	G
	E3		fx {=TABLE(,B2)}				
	A	B	C	D	Payment amount	Total payments	Total interest
1	Loan amount:	$100,000.00		4.50%	$506.69	$182,406.71	$82,406.71
2	Interest rate:	4.50%		4.75%	$521.65	$187,793.04	$87,793.04
3	Payment period (months):	1		5.00%	$536.82	$193,255.78	$93,255.78
4	Number of periods:	360		5.25%	$552.20	$198,793.33	$98,793.33
5				5.50%	$567.79	$204,404.04	$104,404.04
6	Payment amount:	$506.69		5.75%	$583.57	$210,086.23	$110,086.23
7	Total payments:	$182,406.71		6.00%	$599.55	$215,838.19	$115,838.19
8	Total interest:	$82,406.71		6.25%	$615.72	$221,658.19	$121,658.19
9				6.50%	$632.07	$227,544.49	$127,544.49
10							

To create a one-way data table:

1. In the first row of the data table, enter the formulas that return the results.

   In this example, the interest rate varies in the data table, and the interest rate that you actually use for the formulas (in cell B2) is irrelevant because it will be replaced in the data table. Here, the first row of the data table is E2:G2, and the formulas in these cells refer to other formulas in column B: E2 contains =B6, F2 contains =B7, and G2 contains =B8.

2. In the first column of the data table, enter various values for a single input cell.

    In this example, the input value is an interest rate, and cells D2:D10 contain various candidate rates. The first row of the data table (row 2) displays the results for the first input value (in cell D2).

3. Select the range that contains the table entries.

    Here, select D2:G10.

4. In Excel 2007 or later, choose Data tab > Data Tools group (or Forecast group) > What-If Analysis > Data Table. In Excel 2003 or earlier, choose Data menu > Table.

    The Data Table dialog box opens.

    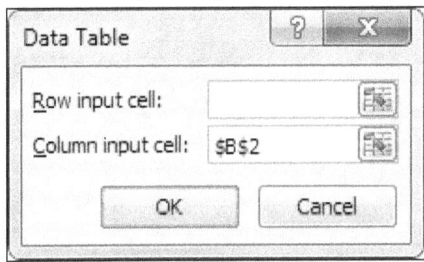

5. In the "Column input cell" field, type the cell reference that corresponds to the input variable.

    Here, the column input cell is B2.

6. Leave the "Row input cell" field empty, and click OK.

    Excel inserts an array formula (page 3) that uses the TABLE function with one argument. The array formula doesn't include first column and first row of your selection in step 3—those values remain unchanged.

    Format the data table as desired.

Two-Way Data Tables

A **two-way data table** shows the results of a single calculation for different values of two input cells. The following figure shows the layout of a two-way data table.

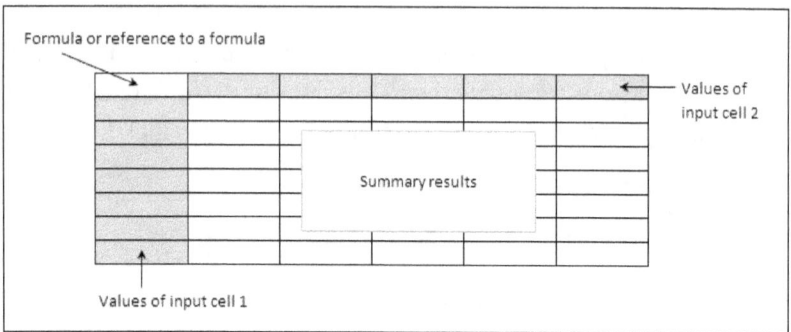

The following figure shows a two-way data table (in A8:G15) that displays a calculation (payment amount) for a 30-year mortgage, using six different interest rates ranging from 4.5% to 5.75%, and seven loan amounts ranging from $100,000 to $250,000. The input cells are B2 and B1.

	A	B	C	D	E	F	G
		B9	fx {=TABLE(B2,B1)}				
1	Loan amount:	$100,000.00					
2	Interest rate:	4.50%					
3	Payment period (months):	1					
4	Number of periods:	360					
5	Payment amount:	$506.69					
6							
7							
8	$506.69	4.50%	4.75%	5.00%	5.25%	5.50%	5.75%
9	$100,000.00	$506.69	$521.65	$536.82	$552.20	$567.79	$583.57
10	$125,000.00	$633.36	$652.06	$671.03	$690.25	$709.74	$729.47
11	$150,000.00	$760.03	$782.47	$805.23	$828.31	$851.68	$875.36
12	$175,000.00	$886.70	$912.88	$939.44	$966.36	$993.63	$1,021.25
13	$200,000.00	$1,013.37	$1,043.29	$1,073.64	$1,104.41	$1,135.58	$1,167.15
14	$225,000.00	$1,140.04	$1,173.71	$1,207.85	$1,242.46	$1,277.53	$1,313.04
15	$250,000.00	$1,266.71	$1,304.12	$1,342.05	$1,380.51	$1,419.47	$1,458.93

To create a two-way data table:

1. In the top-left cell of the data table, enter a formula that returns the results that you want to use in the data table.

   In this example, the formula in cell A8 is =B5, which refers to the payment calculation.

2. Enter various values for the first input in successive columns of the first row of the data table.

   Here, the first input value is the interest rate, and the values for various interest rates are in B8:G8.

3. Enter various values for the second input cell in successive rows of the first column of the data table.

   Here, the second input value is the loan amount, and the values for various loan amounts are in A9:A15.

4. Select the range that contains the table entries.

   Here, select A8:G15.

5. In Excel 2007 or later, choose Data tab > Data Tools group (or Forecast group) > What-If Analysis > Data Table. In Excel 2003 or earlier, choose Data menu > Table.

   The Data Table dialog box opens.

   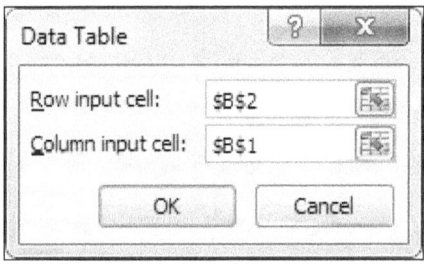

6. In the "Row input cell" field, type the cell reference that corresponds to the first input variable.

   Here, the row input cell is B2.

7. In the "Column input cell" field, type the cell reference that corresponds to the second input variable.

   Here, the column input cell is B1.

8. Click OK.

   Excel inserts an array formula (page 3) that uses the TABLE function with two arguments. Format the data table as desired.

You can change the formula in the top-left cell of the data table to a different calculation. To make the table display total interest rather than payment amounts, for example, change the formula in cell A8 to:

=PMT(B2*(B3/12),B4,-B1)*B4-B1

11 Getting Started with Dates & Times

Calculations with dates and times are among the most common spreadsheet operations, and Excel's capabilities go far beyond routine TODAY and DATE formulas. Part II (Chapters 11–15) of this book shows you how to use worksheet functions, array formulas, Auto-Fill, and other Excel features to work with date and time values. If you're using an older version of Excel that doesn't support the latest worksheet functions, then you'll find equivalent formulas that work in Excel 2003 or earlier.

- Enter and format dates and times quickly.
- Understand date serial numbers and time serial numbers.
- Enter dates and times in various formats.
- Combine or format dates and times.
- Handle problem dates.
- Master the Date & Time functions.
- Use advanced date formulas and time formulas.

Downloading the Sample Workbook

To follow along with or copy the examples in this book, download the Excel workbook excel_dates_times.xlsx from *questingvolepress.com* (a .xls workbook is also included for pre-2007 versions of Excel). This workbook contains worksheets that demonstrate most of the example formulas.

Tip: If you're using Excel 2007 or later and sharing your workbooks with people using earlier versions of Excel, then read the Microsoft support article, "Save an Excel workbook for compatibility with earlier versions of Excel" at *support.office.com*.

	A	B	C	D	E
1	start_date	end_date	unit	result	notes
2	1/1/2012	3/15/2013	m	14	Complete months
3	1/1/2012	3/15/2013	d	439	Days
4	1/1/2012	3/15/2013	y	1	Complete years
5	1/1/2012	3/15/2013	ym	2	Months, ignoring years
6	1/1/2012	3/15/2013	yd	74	Days, ignoring years
7	1/1/2012	3/15/2013	md	14	Days, ignoring months and years

Using the Example Formulas

When you adapt the example formulas in this book to use in your own Excel workbooks, keep the following issues in mind.

Named Ranges

Some example formulas use **named ranges** as function arguments: MONTH(due_date) or SUM(values), for example. When you use these formulas in your own worksheets, substitute either the actual range reference (A1:E8, for example) or a range name defined in your workbook (Formulas tab > Defined Names group > Name Manager).

If your data are in a table, then you can use table referencing in your formulas instead of creating named ranges. For example, if a table named Table1 has a column named Sales, then you can enter

```
=COUNTIFS(Table1[Sales],">=500",Table1[Sales],
"<=1000")
```

instead of manually creating a range named Sales and entering

```
=COUNTIFS(Sales,">=500",Sales,"<=1000")
```

When you define a range as a table (Insert tab > Tables group > Table), Excel creates names automatically for the table and for each column in the table.

Array Formulas

A formula that's surrounded by braces { } is an **array formula**. For example,

```
{=SUM(IF(ISTEXT(values),1))}
```

Whenever you enter an array formula, you must press Ctrl+Shift+Enter (not just Enter). Don't type the braces manually; they will appear automatically in the formula bar. If you edit an existing array formula, then you must still press Ctrl+Shift+Enter; otherwise, the array formula will revert to a normal formula and return the wrong result. For details, read the Microsoft support article "Guidelines and examples of array formulas" at *support.office.com*.

Circular References

A formula that refers back to its own cell, either directly or indirectly, is a **circular reference**. If the formula =COUNT(A1:C3), for example, is entered in any cell in the range A1:C3, then Excel opens the Circular Reference Warning message box. Circular references are sometimes useful (notably in some financial and scientific calculations) and Excel can solve them iteratively, but they're most often unintentional. For details, read the Microsoft support article "Remove or allow a circular reference" at *support.office.com*.

Entering and Formatting Dates and Times Quickly

Excel offers a few keyboard shortcuts to enter and format dates and times.

Ctrl+;
: Enter the current date.

Ctrl+Shift+:
: Enter the current time.

Ctrl+Shift+#
: Apply the Date format with the day, month, and year.

Ctrl+Shift+@
: Apply the Time format with the hour and minute, and AM or PM.

12 Date & Time Basics

The secret to working with dates and times is understanding how Excel stores and interprets these values. Though dates and times *look* like text values ("June 22, 2013" or "10:30 AM", for example), they're actually serial numbers.

Date Serial Numbers

To Excel, a date is a **serial number**. Excel designates the date January 1, 1900 as day 1; January 2, 1900 is day 2; and so on. This system lets you use dates in formulas. A formula that subtracts one date from another, for example, returns the number of days between the two dates. Technically, a serial number is the number of days since the fictitious date **January 0, 1900** (serial number 0). Excel also uses this nondate for times that aren't associated with a particular day.

Supported Date Ranges

Excel 2000 and later support dates from January 1, 1900 (serial number 1) through December 31, 9999 (serial number 2,958,465).

- If you enter a date outside this range, then Excel treats it as plain text.

- If you format an out-of-range serial number as a date, then Excel displays the cell contents as a series of hash marks (######).

- If you share your workbooks with other people, then keep in mind that Excel 2000 and earlier support dates from January 1, 1900 (serial number 1) through only December 31, 2078 (serial number 65,380).

Days vs. Nights

It's common to refer to the number of *days* between two dates. It's actually clearer and more accurate to refer to the number of *nights*, since that's what's actually being counted. Night-counting is what banks use to calculate interest. If you deposit money and then withdraw it the next day, for example, then the bank pays you interest for only one night, not two days. If you deposit and then later withdraw money on the same day, then you earn no interest (zero nights).

1904 Date System

Excel supports an alternate date system that designates January 1, 1904 as day 1. This format ensures compatibility with the Mac OS X version of Excel, which by default uses the **1904 date system**. To change your workbook to use January 1, 1904 as the base date, choose File tab > Options > Advanced section (on the left) > select "Use 1904 date system" (under "When calculating this workbook"). The dates in your workbook won't change visibly, but their internal representations change. If you enter a date earlier than January 1, 1904, then Excel converts it to plain text. (You can't change the date system in Excel for Mac).

In general, use the default 1900 date system. If you transfer workbooks between Windows and Mac, then Excel is smart enough to account for the different date systems, but other problems exist. If you have two workbooks that use different date systems, for example, then copying-and-pasting or linking between them can cause the same date serial number to be interpreted differently. Also, using the General cell format for dates can cause errors if you transfer workbooks.

The 1904 date system offers one advantage: it can display negative time values. In the 1900 date system, Excel can't display a calculation that returns a negative time: 7:00 AM minus 9:30 AM, for example. In the 1904 date system, Excel shows the negative time as −2:30 (a difference of two hours and 30 minutes).

All examples in this book use the 1900 date system.

Entering Dates

You can enter a date directly as a serial number, but almost no one does so—you can use Excel happily for years never knowing or seeing dates' underlying serial numbers. Ordinarily, you enter a date by typing it in a valid date format (*1/1/2012*, for example). Excel converts your entry automatically to the corresponding date serial number and formats it as an easily readable date rather than as a serial number. Excel uses the serial number, not the formatted date text, for calculations.

If you type *22-June-2012*, for example, then Excel converts it to the value (serial number) 41082 and applies a date format according to your Windows settings. The cell contents might not appear exactly as you typed them.

When you select a cell that contains a date, the formula bar shows the cell contents in the default date format, which is your system's **short date** format. To see a date's underlying serial number, change to General format: right-click the cell and then choose Format Cells > Number tab > General category, or select the cell and then press Ctrl+Shift+~.

	A	B
1	Date	Format
2	6/22/2012	Short date
3	Friday, June 22, 2012	Long date
4	41082	General (internal representation)

Changing the Default Date Format

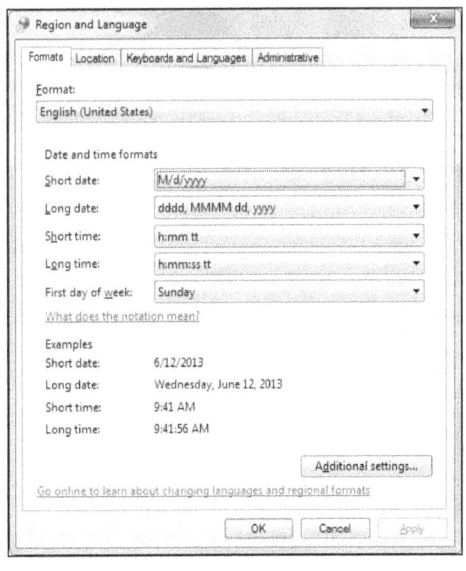

To change the default date format that Excel uses, you must change the systemwide setting for Windows. In Windows, choose Control Panel > Region (or Region and Language) > Formats tab > "Short date" drop-down list. A **long date** format is also available.

Day, Month, and Year Order

For this book, the regional format is "English (United States)", so short dates appear in **month-day-year** order (5-1-2012 is May 1, 2012—not January 5, 2012). Most other countries use **day-month-year** order and regard the U.S. standard as illogical. Programmers, however, consider both of these formats to be inferior to **year-month-day** with a four-digit year, two-digit month, and two-digit day (2012-05-01). A list of dates in YMD format sorts accurately (chronologically) as text, which is handy if you paste a column of dates into a text file or other document.

Date Examples

The following examples show how Excel interprets and displays dates entered in various **date formats** (for default "English (United States)" settings).

6/22/12
> Displays 6/22/2012 (Windows short date).

6/22/2012
> Displays 6/22/2012 (Windows short date).

6-22-12
> Displays 6/22/2012 (Windows short date).

6-22-2012
> Displays 6/22/2012 (Windows short date).

6/22-12
> Displays 6/22/2012 (Windows short date).

June 22, 2012
> Displays 22-Jun-12.

Jun 22
> Displays 22-Jun (of current year).

June 22
> Displays 22-Jun (of current year).

6/22
> Displays 22-Jun (of current year).

6-22
: Displays 22-Jun (of current year).

22-Jun-12
: Displays 22-Jun-12.

2012/6/22
: Displays 6/22/2012.

June 22,2012
: Not recognized as a date because there's no space between the comma and the number 2012. Values are interpreted and displayed as text, which can't be used in date formulas.

Jun 22 2012, Jun/22/2012, and *June-22-2012*
: Not recognized as dates. Values are interpreted and displayed as text, which can't be used in date formulas.

6/22/1865 and *22-Jun-10012*
: Falls outside of the supported date range. Values are interpreted and displayed as text, which can't be used in date formulas. If you format an out-of-range serial number as a date, then Excel displays the cell contents as a series of hash marks (######).

Searching for Dates

To search for dates on a worksheet, press Ctrl+F (or choose Home tab > Editing group > Find & Select list > Find command). In the Find and Replace dialog box that opens, type the date in "Find what" box. Use a four-digit year and the same date format shown in the formula bar.

Time Serial Numbers

For time values, Excel extends date serial numbers to include a decimal portion between 0 and 1, representing the fraction of a day. The date serial number for June 22, 2012, for example, is 41082. Noon (halfway through the day) is represented internally as 41082.5. If a time isn't associated with a particular day, then the integer (whole number) part of the serial number is zero; 0.5 is noon, for example. Simple arithmetic yields common fractions of a day:

- The fraction for one hour is about 0.041666667, which equals 1/24, or 1 divided by 24 hours.

- The fraction for one minute is about 0.000694444, which equals 1/(24 × 60), or 1 divided by 24 hours times 60 minutes.

- The fraction for one second is about 0.000011574, which equals 1/(24 × 60 × 60), or 1 divided by 24 hours times 60 minutes times 60 seconds.

Here are some examples of times of day and their serial numbers:

12:00 AM (midnight, the start of the day)
    0.0000 (0/24).

1:30 AM
    0.0625 (1.5/24).

3:00 AM
    0.1250 (3/24).

6:00 AM
    0.2500 (6/24).

10:30 AM
    0.4375 (10.5/24).

12:00 PM (noon)
    0.5000 (12/24).

1:30 PM
    0.5625 (13.5/24).

9:00 PM
    0.8750 (21/24).

10:30 PM
    0.9375 (22.5/24).

Time Precision

Times are precise to eight decimal places, or about one **millisecond** (one one-thousandth of a second). A millisecond before midnight

(11:59:59.999 PM) is the serial number 0.99999999. The fraction for one millisecond is about 1.15741E–08, which equals 1/(24 × 60 × 60 × 1000).

Entering Times

Entering times is just like entering dates because the date and time are just different components of a single number. As with dates, you don't have to enter actual serial numbers (though you can if you like). Instead, enter a time by typing it in a valid time format. The default **short time** and **long time** formats are set in Control Panel's Region (or Region and Language) dialog box.

	A	B
1	Time	Format
2	10:30:00 AM	Long time
3	10:30	Short time
4	0.4375	General (internal representation)

Time Examples

The following examples show how Excel interprets and displays times entered in various **time formats** (for default "English (United States)" settings).

10:30:00 am or *10:30:00 a*
  Displays 10:30:00 AM (Windows long time).

10:30:00 AM or *10:30:00 A*
  Displays 10:30:00 AM (Windows long time).

10:30 pm or *10:30 p*
  Displays 10:30 PM.

10:30
  Displays 10:30 (interpreted as 10:30 AM).

14:30
  Displays 14:30 (2:30 PM).

10 pm
  Displays 10:00 PM.

January 0, 1900

The preceding examples aren't associated with a specific day, so Excel uses zero for the date portion of the serial number. Zero corresponds to the fictitious date January 0, 1900. If you format the time 10:30 AM (serial number 0.4375) as a date, for example, then the formula bar shows 1/0/1900 10:30:00 AM.

Tip: If you're using the 1904 date system, then time values without an explicit date use January 1, 1904 as the date.

Combining Dates and Times

To combine a date and time, type a date in a valid date format, followed by a space, followed by a time in a valid time format. If you type *6/22/2012 10:30* in a cell, for example, then Excel interprets it as 10:30 AM on June 22, 2012. Its date/time serial number is 41082.4375.

	A	B
1	Date/time	Internal representation
2	6/22/2012	41082
3	10:30	0.4375
4	6/22/2012 10:30	41082.4375

A few caveats:

- If you enter a time that exceeds 24 hours, then the associated date increments (recall that a time entered without a date uses January 0, 1900 as the date). If you type *30:00* in a cell, for example, then it's interpreted as 6:00 AM on January 1, 1900 (30 hours = 1 day + 6 hours). Similarly, *50:00* is interpreted as 2:00 AM on January 2, 1900 (50 hours = 2 days + 2 hours).

- If you enter a date *and* a time (and the time exceeds 24 hours), then the date increments. If you type *6/22/2012 30:00* in a cell, for example, then it's interpreted as 6:00 AM on June 23, 2012.

- The **maximum time** (with no associated date) that you can enter in a cell is 9999:59:59 (a smidge under 10,000 hours or 416.67 days).

9999:59:59 is interpreted as 3:59:59 PM on February 19, 1901. If you enter a time that exceeds 10,000 hours, then it's interpreted and displayed as text (which can't be used in date/time formulas).

Formatting Dates and Times

You can format cells that contain dates and times to show the date part only, the time part only, or both parts. Formatting a date/time cell in General format (Ctrl+Shift+~) shows the serial number. To format cells, select them and then apply a format. The Number Format drop-down list (Home tab > Number group) offers some common date/time formats.

For a larger selection of formats, including custom formats, use the Format Cells dialog box. To open it, press Ctrl+1; click More Number Formats in the Number Format list (shown above); or click Dialog box launcher in the bottom-right corner of the Number group (on the Home tab). Choose a format in the Date or Time categories, or select the Custom category and then type custom format codes in the Type box.

A useful custom format for displaying times is *[h]:mm:ss*. The square brackets make Excel display hours beyond 24 hours. For details, see "Summing Times" on page 95.

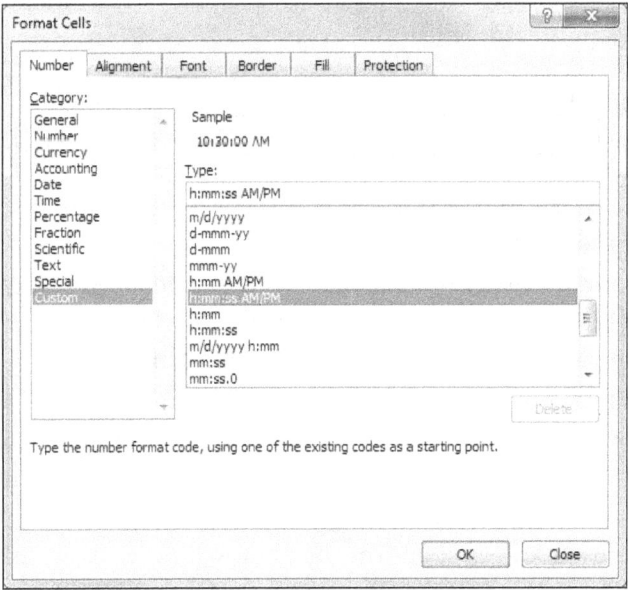

Tip: If you format a date/time to hide part of its information, then Excel still uses the cell's entire value in calculations.

Autoformatted Date and Time Formulas

When you create a formula that refers to a cell containing a date or time, Excel might autoformat the formula cell itself as a date or time, which is either helpful or irritating depending on the result of the formula. You can't disable autoformatting but you can quickly remove all number formatting from the selected cell(s) by applying the General format with a keyboard shortcut: Ctrl+Shift+~.

Keyboard Shortcuts for Formatting

A few keyboard shortcuts to quickly format selected dates and times:

- To format dates as *d-mmm-yy* (22-Jun-12, for example), press Ctrl+Shift+#.

- To format times as *h:mm AM/PM* (10:30 AM, for example), press Ctrl+Shift+@.

- To format dates or times in General format (that is, as serial numbers), press Ctrl+Shift+~.

Problem Dates

Excel has date-related problems stemming from choices made by Excel's original designers.

The Leap Year Bug

A **leap year**, which occurs every four years, contains an extra day (February 29). Years evenly divisible by 100 aren't leap years unless they're also evenly divisible by 400. The bug: Excel treats 1900 as a leap year even though it isn't one. When you type *2/29/1900* in a cell, Excel wrongly interprets it as a valid date and converts it to the date serial number 60. By contrast, *2/29/1901* is correctly interpreted as a non-existent date and formatted as plain text.

Microsoft knows about this bug but will never fix it. Excel was originally designed to be compatible with Lotus 1-2-3, the dominant spreadsheet program at the time. Lotus 1-2-3 contained this bug, and Excel's designers chose to reproduce it to be compatible with Lotus files. Sad but true. The consequences:

- Date calculations that span February 29, 1900 will be off by one day.
- Days of the week (Sunday, Monday,...) prior to March 1, 1900 are wrong.
- We're stuck with this bug. Fixing it would change the internal numbering of every date after February 28, 1900, breaking possibly millions of existing spreadsheets that use dates. A fix would also break compatibility between Excel and other programs that use dates.

Fortunately, this problem is fairly benign because most users don't use dates before March 1, 1900.

See also "Determining Whether a Year is a Leap Year" on page 89.

Two-Digit Years

Be careful when entering dates by using only the last two digits of the year. When you do so, Excel determines which century to use by looking at your Windows system settings.

By default, two-digit years between 00 and 29 are interpreted as 21st century years, and 30–99 are interpreted as 20th century years. *12/10/29*, for example, is interpreted as December 10, 2029, and *12/10/30* is interpreted as December 10, 1930. To change the boundary year that Excel uses, you must change the systemwide setting for Windows. In Windows, choose Control Panel > Region (or Region and Language) > Formats tab > "Additional settings" button > Date tab > Calendar section.

Best practice: enter every year by typing all four digits.

Dates Before 1900

Excel's world starts on January 1, 1900 (date serial number 1). Negative serial numbers aren't allowed. The only way to work with pre-1900 dates is to enter them as text. Sadly, you can't use date formulas on dates recognized as text.

If all you need to do is sort by date, then enter old dates as text in year-month-day format with a four-digit year, two-digit month, and two-digit day (1789-07-14, for example). A list of dates in this format sorts accurately (chronologically). Alternatively, you can split dates into three columns (year, month, and day), which lets you do math operations on the separate numeric values (though sorting then becomes a multilevel operation).

You can also search online for specific solutions. The Microsoft support article "How to calculate ages before 1/1/1900 in Excel" at *support.microsoft.com*, for example, gives a VBA macro that calculates a person's age from pre-1900 birth and death dates.

Tip: Dates in or before September 1752 lack a standard calendar. For details, see *wikipedia.org/wiki/Gregorian_calendar#Adoption*.

Text That Looks Like a Date or Time

If you want Excel to treat a date- or time-like string as plain text (that is, not convert it to a serial number), then type a leading apostrophe (single quote) in the cell before the text (*'6/22/2012*, for example). A leading apostrophe tells Excel to treat an entry as text even if it recognizes it as a date or time.

13 Date & Time Functions

Excel's date and time functions are listed under Formulas tab > Function Library group > Date & Time list.

Tip: In Excel 2003 or earlier, you must load the Analysis ToolPak add-in to access all the date and time functions. To do so, choose Tools menu > Add-Ins > select Analysis ToolPak > OK.

TODAY and NOW: Inserting the Current Date and Time

The **TODAY** function returns the current date, retrieved from your computer's internal clock. TODAY takes no arguments:

```
TODAY()
```

You can display the current date in a cell:

```
=TODAY()
```

Or combine it with text:

```
="Today is " & TEXT(TODAY(),"ddd, yyyy-mmm-d")
```

TODAY is updated whenever the worksheet is calculated. For example, if cell A1 contains the date that a payment was due, then

```
=TODAY()-A1
```

returns the current number of days that the payment is late. The result is an ordinary number, not a date serial number. If Excel autoformats the cell as a date, then manually format it in General format (Ctrl+Shift+~).

The **NOW** function is similar to TODAY, except it returns the current date *and* the current time. NOW takes no arguments:

```
NOW()
```

You can display the current date/time in a cell:

```
=NOW()
```

Or combine it with text:

```
="The current date and time is " & TEXT(NOW(),
"ddd, yyyy-mmm-d h:mm AM/PM")
```

The current time without an associated date is

```
=NOW()-TODAY()
```

You can manually format cells to show only the parts of a date/time that you want to display.

Entering Static Dates and Times

To quickly enter the current date as a **static value** (which never changes) in a cell, press Ctrl+; (semicolon). To enter the current time as a static value, press Ctrl+Shift+; (semicolon). Static values are also called **literals**.

To convert the result of a formula to a static value, select the formula cell, press F2 to enter edit mode, press F9 to replace the formula with its calculated result, and then press Enter.

DATE and TIME: Inserting Any Date or Time

You can type a single date into a cell, but you can't use the same syntax to insert a date in a formula. For example, Excel doesn't interpret

```
=3/3/2012-2/2/2011
```
  (Wrong)

to be the number of days between March 3, 2012 and February 2, 2011. Rather, Excel sees the entire formula as one long arithmetic expression—the slashes are treated as division operators, not date separators. You *can* insert literal dates in formulas by typing serial numbers, but the resulting formulas are cryptic and hard to debug (the "corrected" version of the preceding formula is `=40971-40576`).

Instead, use the DATE function enter a literal date value in a formula. DATE takes the three components of a date:

DATE(*year, month, day*)

and returns the date's serial number. For example,

=DATE(2012,6,22)

displays 6/22/2012 (or the serial number 41082, depending on the cell's format). DATE accepts nonstandard arguments and shifts the returned date accordingly:

- If *year* is between 0 and 1899 (inclusive), then DATE adds that value to 1900 to calculate the year. For example, =DATE(112,6,22) returns June 22, 2012 (1900 plus 112 years). To avoid errors, always use a four-digit year.

- If *month* is greater than 12, then DATE adds that number of months to the first month of *year*. For example, =DATE(2012,15,5) returns March 5, 2013 (January 5, 2012 plus 15 months).

- If *month* is less than 1, then DATE subtracts the magnitude of that number of months, plus 1, from the first month of *year*. For example, =DATE(2012,-3,5) returns September 5, 2011 (January 5, 2012 minus 4 months).

- If *day* exceeds the number of days in *month*, then DATE adds that number of days to the first day of *month*. For example, =DATE(2012,6,45) returns July 15, 2012 (June 1, 2012 plus 45 days).

- If *day* is less than 1, then DATE subtracts the magnitude of that number of days, plus 1, from the first day of *month*. For example, =DATE(2012,6,-15) returns May 16, 2012 (June 1, 2012 minus 16 days).

DATE is generally used as an expression or a function argument in a formula. The following formula returns the number of days between 1/1/2010 and the date in cell A1:

=A1-DATE(2010,1,1)

The TIME function works similarly with time values. It takes the three components of a time:

TIME(hour, minute, second)

and returns the time's serial number. Enter hours by using a 24-hour clock. You can use fractional seconds to indicate milliseconds.

For example,

=TIME(21,0,0)

displays 9:00 PM (or the serial number 0.875, depending on the cell's format).

Like DATE, TIME accepts nonstandard arguments and shifts the returned time accordingly:

- *hour* is between 0 and 32767 (inclusive). If *hour* is greater than 23, then TIME "wraps around" the 24-hour clock. For example, =TIME(27,0,0) is equivalent to =TIME(3,0,0) (3:00 AM or 0.125). Technically, this wrap-around operation is *modular arithmetic*: any *hour* greater than 23 is divided by 24 and the remainder is treated as the hour value.

- *minute* is between 0 to 32767 (inclusive). Any value greater than 59 is converted to hours and minutes. For example, =TIME(0,630,0) is equivalent to =TIME(10,30,0) (10:30 AM or 0.4375).

- *second* is between 0 to 32767 (inclusive). Any value greater than 59 is converted to hours, minutes, and seconds. For example, =TIME(0,0,16245) is equivalent to =TIME(4,30,45) (4:30:45 AM or 0.188020833).

The following formula returns the date/time value for 10:30 AM on June 22, 2012 (serial number 41082.4375):

=DATE(2012,6,22)+TIME(10,30,0)

If cell A1 contains a time, then the following formula adds four hours and 30 minutes to it:

=A1+TIME(4,30,0)

The following formula calculates how much time between now and midnight:

`=TIME(23,59,59.999)-(NOW()-TODAY())`

The expression NOW()-TODAY() removes the date portion of the current date/time. The final result is expressed as a fractional number of days. You can format the cell as a time (or multiply by 24 to convert to hours).

DAY, MONTH, and YEAR: Extracting Part of a Date

The DAY, MONTH, and YEAR functions return the day, month, and year of a given date.

DAY(*serial_number*)

MONTH(*serial_number*)

YEAR(*serial_number*)

Each function takes a date serial number and returns a number representing the day (1 to 31), the month (1 to 12), or the year (1900 to 9999), respectively. For example, if cell A1 contains the date 6/22/2012, then =DAY(A1) returns 22, =MONTH(A1) returns 6, and =YEAR(A1) returns 2012.

To use DAY, MONTH, and YEAR with a date literal, use the DATE function as the argument. For example,

`=MONTH(DATE(2012,6,22))`

returns 6.

Tip: The formulas =MONTH(6/22/2012) and =MONTH(6-22-2012) won't return the values that you expect because MONTH's argument must be a date serial number. Here, Excel passes the result of the division 6/22/2012 (which is 0.00013555) or the subtraction 6-22-2012 (which is -2028) to the MONTH function, which returns a meaningless answer or an error.

DAY, MONTH, and YEAR are often used with DATE to calculate dates that fall a fixed number of periods before or after a specific date. For example,

```
=DATE(YEAR(A1),MONTH(A1),DAY(A1)+14)
```

returns the date that's 14 days after the date in cell A1.
Two years before the date in cell A1 is

```
=DATE(YEAR(A1)-2,MONTH(A1),DAY(A1))
```

Equivalently, 24 months before is

```
=DATE(YEAR(A1),MONTH(A1)-24,DAY(A1))
```

Christmas Day (December 25) of the current year is

```
=DATE(YEAR(TODAY()),12,25)
```

To flag the first day of the month, use

```
=IF(DAY(TODAY())=1,
"Today is the first of the month","")
```

See also "Basic Date Arithmetic" on page 85.

SECOND, MINUTE, and HOUR: Extracting Part of a Time

The **SECOND**, **MINUTE**, and **HOUR** functions work like DAY, MONTH, and YEAR, except that they return the number of seconds, minutes, and hours in a given time.

SECOND(*serial_number*)

MINUTE(*serial_number*)

HOUR(*serial_number*)

Each function takes a time serial number and returns a number representing the second (0 to 59), the minute (0 to 59), or the hour (0 to 23), respectively. For example, if cell A1 contains the time 10:30 PM, then =SECOND(A1) returns 0, =MINUTE(A1) returns 30, and =HOUR(A1) returns 22 (HOUR uses a 24-hour clock).

To use SECOND, MINUTE, and HOUR with a time literal, use the TIME function as the argument. For example,

    =MINUTE(TIME(22,30,0))

returns 30.

See also "Basic Time Arithmetic" on page 95.

DATEVALUE and TIMEVALUE: Converting Text to a Date or Time

DATEVALUE and TIMEVALUE convert dates and times in the form of text to serial numbers.

    DATEVALUE(date_text)

    TIMEVALUE(time_text)

These functions can convert text in any recognizable date format or time format. For example, DATEVALUE can convert *March 4, 1960* and *6-22-2012*, but not *March 4th, 1960* or *6 22 2012*.

DATEVALUE and TIMEVALUE ignore an initial apostrophe (single quote) in a text value. For example, if cell A1 contains the text value *'6/22/2012*, then

    =DATEVALUE(A1)

returns the serial number 41082.

These function also work with date and time literals. The formula

    =TIMEVALUE("10:30 AM")

returns the serial number 0.4375.

Tip: The text strings that DATEVALUE and TIMEVALUE recognize depend on your settings in Control Panel's Region (or Region and Language) dialog box.

See also "Converting Text to Dates" on page 88 and "Converting Text to Times" on page 98.

WEEKDAY: Determining the Day of the Week

WEEKDAY takes a date serial number, and returns a number that represents which day of the week that date falls on (1 = Sunday, 2 = Monday,..., 7 = Saturday).

WEEKDAY(*serial_number,* [*return_type*])

The optional second argument, *return_type*, is a number (integer) that determines the day numbering system. If *return_type* is 1 or omitted, then WEEKDAY uses the numbering system described above. If *return_type* is 2, then WEEKDAY returns 1 for Monday, 2 for Tuesday, and so on. If *return_type* is 3, then WEEKDAY returns 0 for Monday, 1 for Tuesday, and so on. Other values of *return_type* let you start counting on any day of the week.

For example,

=WEEKDAY(DATE(2012,6,22))

returns 6 (Friday).

You can show the day's name instead of its number:

=TEXT(WEEKDAY(DATE(2012,6,22)),"dddd")

returns the full day name (*Friday*), and

=TEXT(WEEKDAY(DATE(2012,6,22)),"ddd")

returns the day's three-letter abbreviation (*Fri*).

Tip: You can also determine the day of the week for a cell that contains a date by applying the custom format code *dddd* or *ddd* to the cell.

DAYS360: Counting Days Between Two Accounting Dates

DAYS360 counts the number of days between two dates. Unlike simple date subtraction, DAYS360 assumes that every month has 30 days (a 360-day year). This calendar is commonly used in accounting, payroll, and financial systems.

DAYS360(*start_date, end_date,* [*method*])

Normally, the earlier date goes first, followed by the later date. If you want DAYS360 to return a negative number, then swap the two date arguments.

The third argument, *method*, is an optional logical value that changes the day-count method if *start_date* or *end_date* falls on the 31st day of the month.

- If *method* is FALSE or omitted, then the U.S. NASD (National Association of Securities Dealers) day-counting method is used. If *start_date* is 31, then it's changed to 30. If *end_date* is 31, then it's handled differently depending on *start_date*. If *start_date* is 30 or 31, then *end_date* changes to day 30 in the same month. If *start_date* is less than 30, then *end_date* changes from 31 to day 1 of the next month.

- If *method* is TRUE, then the European day-counting method is used: both a *start_date* and *end_date* of 31 are changed to 30.

For example,

=DAYS360(DATE(2013,2,1),DATE(2013,3,1))

returns 30 (in the DAYS360 calendar, February has 30 days).

EDATE: Adding and Subtracting Months

EDATE adds or subtracts a specified number of months to or from a given date.

EDATE(*start_date, months*)

A positive number of *months* moves forward from *start_date*, and a negative number moves backward. For example, the following formula returns the date serial number one month from today:

=EDATE(TODAY(),1)

Six months ago:

=EDATE(TODAY(),-6)

EDATE accounts for leap years:

=EDATE(DATE(2012,1,31),1)

returns February 29, 2012.

EDATE can't offset dates by days or years. If that's what you need, then use DAY, MONTH, and YEAR.

Tip: If Excel autoformats an EDATE result as a serial number, then manually format it as a date.

YEARFRAC: Calculating the Fraction of a Year Between Two Dates

YEARFRAC calculates the number of years between two dates, including partial (fractional) years. If you pay an annual fee to your knitting club, then you can use YEARFRAC to calculate a prorated refund if you quit the club partway through the year.

YEARFRAC(*start_date, end_date,* [*basis*])

The start and end dates can fall in the same year or in different years. The optional third argument, *basis*, is used for financial applications and determines how Excel should calculate the fraction. *basis* is a number (integer) from 0 to 4:

- 0 or omitted (US NASD 30/360). YEARFRAC mimics the DAYS360 function.

- 1 (Actual/actual). The actual number of days between the two dates is divided by the actual number of days in the year, accounting for leap years.

- 2 (Actual/360). The actual number of days between the two dates is divided by 360.

- 3 (Actual/365). The actual number of days between the two dates is divided by 365 (returning the same answer as basis 1 if the year isn't a leap year).

- 4 (European 30/360). YEARFRAC mimics the European version of DAYS360.

The following formula calculates the fraction of the year between January 1, 2012 and April 1, 2012:

=YEARFRAC(DATE(2012,1,1),DATE(2012,4,1),1)

The result is 0.24863388, or about 25 percent, of the year.

EOMONTH: Finding the Last Day of a Month

EOMONTH calculates the last day of any month in the past or future. It's designed for business people who want to create end-of-month payment, invoice, or maturity schedules.

EOMONTH(*start_date, months*)

A positive number of *months* moves forward from *start_date*, and a negative number moves backward. For example,

=EOMONTH(DATE(2012,6,22),3)

returns September 30, 2012 (three months hence), and

=EOMONTH(DATE(2012,6,22),-12)

returns June 30, 2011 (12 months ago).

The last day of the current month is

=EOMONTH(TODAY(),0)

The number of days in the current month is

=DAY(EOMONTH(TODAY(),0))

EOMONTH accounts for leap years:

=EOMONTH(DATE(2012,1,1),1)

returns February 29, 2012.

Tip: If Excel autoformats an EOMONTH result as a serial number, then manually format it as a date.

NETWORKDAYS: Counting Business Days

NETWORKDAYS counts the number of business days between two dates. Weekends (Saturday and Sunday) are excluded automatically. You can optionally supply a list of holidays not to count.

NETWORKDAYS(start_date, end_date, [holidays])

The following formula returns 21, the number of working days in December 2012:

=NETWORKDAYS(DATE(2012,12,1), DATE(2012,12,31))

You can specify *holidays* in a few ways. To specify one holiday, you can use the DATE function:

=NETWORKDAYS(DATE(2012,12,1), DATE(2012,12,31), DATE(2012,12,25))

For multiple holidays, you can use an array of literals:

=NETWORKDAYS(DATE(2012,12,1), DATE(2012,12,31), {"12/25/2012", "12/26/2012"})

or a range of cells that contains dates:

=NETWORKDAYS(DATE(2012,12,1), DATE(2012,12,31), C1:C2)

Tip: The NETWORKDAYS.INTL function, available in Excel 2010 or later, is an international version of NETWORKDAYS that counts business days when weekends are days other than Saturday and Sunday.

WORKDAY: Offsetting a Date by a Number of Business Days

WORKDAY offsets a given date by a specified number of business days. Weekends (Saturday and Sunday) are skipped automatically. You can optionally supply a list of holidays to skip. WORKDAY is often used to calculate payment, invoice, maturity, or delivery dates.

WORKDAY(start_date, days, [holidays])

A positive number of *days* moves forward from *start_date*, and a negative number moves backward. To specify *holidays*, see NETWORKDAYS.

The following formula returns the date that falls 30 business days after the current date:

```
=WORKDAY(TODAY(),30)
```

Tip: The WORKDAY.INTL function, available in Excel 2010 or later, is an international version of WORKDAY that offsets business days when weekends are days other than Saturday and Sunday.

WEEKNUM: Calculating the Week Number of a Year

WEEKNUM takes a date and returns a number between 1 and 52 (inclusive) that indicates the week where the date falls in the year.

```
WEEKNUM(serial_number, [return_type])
```

For example,

```
=WEEKNUM(DATE(2012,6,22))
```

returns 25 (the 25th week in the year). By default, the week begins on Sunday. You can specify *return_type* to begin the week on a different day.

Tip: The ISOWEEKNUM function, available in Excel 2013 or later, is an international version of WEEKNUM that calculates the week number according to the ISO 8601 standard.

DATEDIF: Calculating the Difference Between Dates

DATEDIF calculates the number of days, months, or years between two dates. In some versions of Excel, DATEDIF isn't documented in Excel Help, and doesn't appear in the Insert Function dialog box, the Date & Time drop-down list, or the Formula AutoComplete list, meaning you must type it manually. You can find DATEDIF documentation at *support.office.com*.

DATEDIF takes a start date, an end date, and a code that specifies the time unit of interest.

```
DATEDIF(start_date, end_date, unit)
```

start_date must be earlier than *end_date*. *unit* takes one of the following values, which must be enclosed in double quotes:

- "m" (months). The number of complete months between the two dates.
- "d" (days). The number of days between the two dates.
- "y" (years). The number of complete years between the two dates.
- "ym" (months excluding years). The number of complete months between the two dates, as if they were in the same year.
- "yd" (days excluding years). The number of complete days between the two dates, as if they were in the same year.
- "md" (days excluding months and years). The number of complete days between the two dates, as if they were in the same month and the same year. In some cases, this argument might return an inaccurate result. For details, read the Microsoft support article "DATEDIF function" at *support.office.com*.

The number of months between a date in cell A1 and the current date is:

=DATEDIF(TODAY(),A1,"m")

Remember that DATEDIF counts *complete* time intervals. For example,

=DATEDIF(DATE(2012,6,15),DATE(2012,7,15),"m")

returns 1, but

=DATEDIF(DATE(2012,6,15),DATE(2012,7,14),"m")

returns 0 because the interval is a day short of a month.

	A	B	C	D	E
1	start_date	end_date	unit	result	notes
2	1/1/2012	3/15/2013	m		14 Complete months
3	1/1/2012	3/15/2013	d		439 Days
4	1/1/2012	3/15/2013	y		1 Complete years
5	1/1/2012	3/15/2013	ym		2 Months, ignoring years
6	1/1/2012	3/15/2013	yd		74 Days, ignoring years
7	1/1/2012	3/15/2013	md		14 Days, ignoring months and years

14 Date Tricks

Basic Date Arithmetic

Because dates and times are actually numbers, you can use them in arithmetic operations. The most common operation is to subtract one date from another to calculate the number of days (nights, actually) between them. For example, if A1 contains the date 6/15/2012, and A2 contains 7/31/2012, then

    =A2-A1

returns 46. If you subtract a later date from an earlier date, then the result is negative (=A1-A2 returns −46). Note that the result is an ordinary number, not a date serial number. If Excel autoformats the cell as a date, then manually reformat it in General format (Ctrl+Shift+~).

Tip: The DAYS function, available in Excel 2013 or later, also returns the number of days between two dates. Its syntax is DAYS(*end_date, start_date*).

The following formula adds seven days to the date in A1 (6/15/2012):

    =A1+7

The result is 6/22/2012 (serial number 41082).
You can also add a fractional part of a day to a date:

    =A1+7.4375

The result is 6/22/2012 10:30 AM (serial number 41082.4375).

85

Dates and times can also be used as function arguments. For example, if cell A1 contains the date/time 6/22/2012 10:30 AM (serial number 41082.4375), then the following formula extracts only the time, rounded to a whole number of hours:

```
=ROUND((A1-INT(A1))*24,0)
```

The result is 11. The expression A1-INT(A1) removes the date portion of the date/time, leaving only the time portion (0.4375). Multiply by the number of hours in a day (0.4375 × 24 = 10.5) and then round to get a whole number of hours (11).

See also "Basic Time Arithmetic" on page 95.

Generating a Series of Dates

You can use AutoFill to quickly create a series of static dates or use formulas to create a series of custom, dynamic dates.

By Using AutoFill

Excel's AutoFill feature can quickly insert a uniform series of dates in a worksheet (no formulas required). For example, you can create a series of dates, each separated by one month. Or a series of days with weekends omitted. Enter the first date in a cell and then right-drag the cell's fill handle (that is, drag while holding down the right mouse button). Release the mouse button and then choose a command from the shortcut menu.

Tip: The fill handle is the small black square in the lower-right corner of the selection ▢. When you point to the fill handle, the pointer changes to a cross.

The Fill Series command creates series based on multiple starting dates. For example, to create a series of dates separated by seven days, enter the first two dates of the series (say, 1/1/2012 and 1/8/2012). Select both cells, right-drag the cells' fill handle, and then choose Fill Series from the shortcut menu. Excel creates the series by inserting additional dates in seven-day increments.

By Using Formulas

Formulas let you create dynamic date series: change the first date, and the others update automatically (AutoFill, in contrast, creates static series of literal dates). To create a dynamic series, enter the starting date in a cell and then use formulas (copied down the column) to generate additional dates in the series.

For example, to create a series of dates separated by seven days, enter the first date of the series in cell A1, enter

    =A1+7

in cell A2, and then copy this formula down the column as many times as needed.

For a month-separated series, use

`=DATE(YEAR(A1),MONTH(A1)+1,DAY(A1))`

For a year-separated series, use

`=DATE(YEAR(A1)+1,MONTH(A1),DAY(A1))`

For a weekday-only series (assuming that A1 isn't a Saturday or Sunday), use

`=IF(WEEKDAY(A1)=6,A1+3,A1+1)`

See also "Generating a Series of Times" on page 97.

Converting Text to Dates

If you import dates coded as text strings that DATEVALUE can't convert, then you can use Excel's text functions to extract the year, month, and day separately and then use DATE or DATEVALUE to convert these date parts to a date serial number.

For example, a common date format is *yyyymmdd*—a four-digit year followed by a two-digit month, followed by a two-digit day. If cell A1 contains the text value 20120622 (representing June 22, 2012), then

`=DATE(LEFT(A1,4),MID(A1,5,2),RIGHT(A1,2))`

returns 6/22/2012 (serial number 41082). The text functions LEFT, MID, and RIGHT extract the digits of the year, month, and day, respectively.

See also "Converting Text to Times" on page 98.

Converting a Year to Roman Numerals

Excel's ROMAN function converts a year (or any positive integer ≤ 3999) to roman numerals:

`=ROMAN(year)`

For example, `=ROMAN(1938)` returns MCMXXXVIII. The result is text, which can't be used in arithmetic formulas.

Tip: The ARABIC function, available in Excel 2013 or later, converts Roman numerals to Arabic numerals.

Calculating a Person's Age

You can use YEARFRAC or DATEDIF to calculate a person's age (the number of full years that the person has been alive). Either of the following formulas returns the age of the person whose date of birth is in cell A1:

```
=INT(YEARFRAC(TODAY(),A1,1))
=DATEDIF(A1,TODAY(),"y")
```

For extra precision,

```
=DATEDIF(A1,TODAY(),"y") & " years, " &
DATEDIF(A1,TODAY(),"ym") & " months, " &
DATEDIF(A1,TODAY(),"md") & " days"
```

displays a person's age in years, months, and days.

Tip: The formula =INT((TODAY()-A1)/365) doesn't work because it fails to account for leap years. This formula will be off by one year in the days just before or after a person's birthday. Changing 365 to 365.25 (the average number of days in a year) makes the formula more accurate but not perfect.

Determining Whether a Year is a Leap Year

If cell A1 contains a date, then the following formula returns TRUE if that date falls in a leap year; otherwise, it returns FALSE:

```
=IF(MONTH(DATE(YEAR(A1),2,29))=2,TRUE,FALSE)
```

This formula works by determining whether February 29th falls in February (month 2) or March (month 3).

The preceding formula returns TRUE for the year 1900, which is wrong but complies with Excel's leap year bug (page 68). The formula for the true (bug-free) leap year is:

```
=IF(OR(MOD(YEAR(A1),400)=0,AND(MOD(YEAR(A1),4)=0,
MOD(YEAR(A1),100)<>0)),TRUE,FALSE).
```

Determining the Number of Days Remaining in a Year

The number of days remaining in the year from a date in cell A1 is

    =DATE(YEAR(A1),12,31)-A1

The number of days remaining in the year from the current date is

    =DATE(YEAR(TODAY()),12,31)-TODAY()

Tip: The result is an ordinary number, not a date serial number. If Excel autoformats the cell as a date, then manually reformat it in General format (Ctrl+Shift+~).

Determining the Ordinal Day of a Year

Day 1 of the year is January 1, and day 365 (or 366 for a leap year) is December 31. The day number of a date in cell A1 is

    =A1-DATE(YEAR(A1),1,0)

The *day* argument of DATE is zero (the "0th" day of January), which DATE interprets as December 31 of the previous year.

The day number of the current date is

    =TODAY()-DATE(YEAR(TODAY()),1,0)

Tip: The result is an ordinary number, not a date serial number. If Excel autoformats the cell as a date, then manually reformat it in General format (Ctrl+Shift+~).

Determining Which Quarter a Date Falls In

The calendar quarter (1, 2, 3, or 4) for a date in cell A1 is

    =ROUNDUP(MONTH(A1)/3,0)

This formula works by dividing the month number by 3 and then rounding up the result.

Tip: The result is an ordinary number, not a date serial number. If Excel autoformats the cell as a date, then manually reformat it in General format (Ctrl+Shift+~).

If your **fiscal year** doesn't coincide with the calendar year, then you can use the CHOOSE function to calculate the fiscal quarter. For example, if your fiscal year begins in October, then the following formula returns 1 for October, November, and December; 2 for January, February, and March; and so on:

    =CHOOSE(MONTH(A1),2,2,2,3,3,3,4,4,4,1,1,1)

Determining the Previous Weekday

The following formula returns the date of the Sunday immediately preceding the current date. If today is Sunday, then today's date is returned.

    =TODAY()-MOD(TODAY()-1,7)

To return the date for a different day of the week, change the 1 in the formula to 2 (for Monday), 3 (for Tuesday), and so on up to 7 (for Saturday).

Tip: If Excel autoformats the cell as an ordinary number, then manually reformat it as a date.

Determining the Next Weekday

The following formula returns the date of the Sunday that falls immediately after a date in cell A1. If the date in A1 is a Sunday, then that same date is returned.

    =A1+1-WEEKDAY(A1)+7*(1<WEEKDAY(A1))

For example, if cell A1 contains June 22, 2012 (a Friday), then the formula returns June 24, 2012 (the following Sunday).

To return the date for a different day of the week, change both 1's in the formula to 2 (for Monday), 3 (for Tuesday), and so on up to 7 (for Saturday).

Determining the Nth Occurrence of a Weekday in a Month

The following formula (useful for calculating holidays and paydays) returns the date of the *n*th occurrence of a specific weekday in a given month:

```
=DATE(A1,A2,1)+A3-WEEKDAY(DATE(A1,A2,1))+
(A4-(A3>=WEEKDAY(DATE(A1,A2,1))))*7
```

where:

- Cell A1 contains a year (use a four-digit year).

- Cell A2 contains a month number (1 for January, 2 for February, and so on).

- Cell A3 contains a weekday number (1 for Sunday, 2 for Monday, and so on).

- Cell A4 contains an occurrence number of the weekday (1 for the first occurrence of the weekday, 2 for the second occurrence, and so on). If this number exceeds the number of weekdays in the month, then a date from a future month is returned. For example, if you calculate fifth Sunday of June, 2012 (which has only four Sundays), then the first Sunday in July is returned.

To shorten the formula, you can replace cell references with numbers tailored for specific, recurring dates. For example, the following formula returns the date for American Thanksgiving Day (the fourth Thursday in November) for the year in cell A1:

```
=DATE(A1,11,1)+5-WEEKDAY(DATE(A1,11,1))+
(4-(5>=WEEKDAY(DATE(A1,11,1))))*7
```

Canadian Thanksgiving Day (the second Monday of October) is

```
=DATE(A1,10,1)+2-WEEKDAY(DATE(A1,10,1))+
(2-(2>=WEEKDAY(DATE(A1,10,1))))*7
```

Counting Occurrences of a Weekday in a Month

The following formula returns the number of times a specific weekday occurs in a given month. The formula is an array formula (page 57), so you must press Ctrl+Shift+Enter to enter it (don't type the braces {}; they will appear automatically in the formula bar).

```
{=SUM((WEEKDAY(DATE(YEAR(A1),MONTH(A1),
ROW(INDIRECT("1:" & DAY(DATE(YEAR(A1),
MONTH(A1)+1,0))))))=A2)*1)}
```

where:

- Cell A1 contains any date that falls in the month and year of interest.
- Cell A2 contains a weekday number (1 for Sunday, 2 for Monday, and so on).

For example, if cell A1 contains the date June 22, 2012, and cell A2 contains the value 6 (for Friday), then the formula returns 5 (June 2012 contains five Fridays).

Calculating Easter Sunday

Easter Sunday falls on the first Sunday after the next full moon occurs after the vernal equinox. The web is full of cryptic algorithms and formulas—called **computus** procedures—that calculate the date of Easter Sunday. The following formula (which I pass on without explanation) calculates the date of Easter Sunday for the year in cell A1 (use a four-digit year):

```
=FLOOR("5/" & DAY(MINUTE(A1/38)/2+56) & "/" &
A1,7)-34
```

Tip: This formula doesn't work for the 1904 date system (page 60).

15

Time Tricks

Basic Time Arithmetic

Excel's basic arithmetic operators and formats work with time serial numbers, though not always in the ways that you'd expect.

Summing Times

The sum of a series of times that exceeds 24 hours won't display correctly if the cell is misformatted. In the following figure, the range A1:A4 contains times that represent hours and minutes. The formula in cell A5 is =SUM(A1:A4).

	A
1	10:00
2	6:30
3	11:15
4	12:00
5	15:45

The sum shows 15 hours, 45 minutes, but should read 39 hours, 45 minutes (serial number 1.65625). The problem is that cell A5 is formatted to show the time part of the result (0.65625) but not the date part (1). To fix this problem, format cell A5 as *[h]:mm* or *[h]:mm:ss* (the square brackets make Excel display hours beyond 24 hours). Select the cell, press Ctrl+1, choose Number tab > Custom category, and then click a format.

	A
1	10:00
2	6:30
3	11:15
4	12:00
5	39:45

Subtracting Times

You can subtract an earlier time from a later time to get the difference. For example, if cell A1 contains 8:00:00 and cell A2 contains 14:30:00, then the formula =A2-A1 returns 6:30:00 (a difference of six hours and 30 minutes).

If you subtract a later time from an earlier time (=A1-A2, for example), then the result is a negative value, which Excel considers to be an invalid time and displays as a series of hash marks (######) in the cell. Even though a negative time can't be displayed, you can still use it for calculations in other formulas. If the direction of the time difference doesn't matter, then use =ABS(A2-A1) to return the absolute value of the difference.

Negative times usually appear when calculating an elapsed time that spans two days (that is, crosses midnight). For example, if cell A1 contains 20:00 and cell A2 contains 4:00, then =A2-A1 displays ###### instead of eight hours. To fix this problem, use =MOD(A2-A1,1) or =IF(A2<A1,A2+1,A2)-A1.

Tip: The 1904 date system (page 60) can display negative time values.

Offsetting Times

You can offset a time (add or subtract hours) to, say, convert times from Coordinated Universal Time (UTC) to your local **time zone**. To do so, you must know the UTC offset (difference in hours) for your local time zone. For example, Pacific Standard Time (PST) is eight hours earlier than UTC (denoted by UTC−08:00). If cell A1 contains the UTC time, then you *can't* use

    =A1+TIME(-8,0,0)   (*Wrong*)

because TIME doesn't accept negative arguments. Instead, divide −8 by 24 (one hour equals 1/24 of a day) and then add it to UTC. If cell A1 contains the UTC date/time June, 1 2012 6:00 AM, then

    =A1+-8/24

returns May 31, 2012 10:00 PM (note the date change).

Converting Decimal Numbers to Times

To convert a decimal number of hours, minutes, or seconds to a time, simply divide by the number of hours (24), minutes (1440), or seconds (86400) in a day, respectively.

For example, 6.25 hours is 6 hours, 15 minutes (6.25/24 = 06:15:00). 340 minutes is 5 hours, 40 minutes (340/1440 = 05:40:00). 70000 seconds is 19 hours, 26 minutes, 40 seconds (70000/86400 = 19:26:40).

See also "Basic Date Arithmetic" on page 85.

Generating a Series of Times

You can use AutoFill to quickly create a series of static times or use formulas to create a series of custom, dynamic times.

By Using AutoFill

Excel's AutoFill feature can quickly insert a uniform series of times in a worksheet (no formulas required). For example, to create a series of times with 15-minute intervals, enter 9:00 AM in cell A1 and 9:15 AM in cell A2. Select both cells, and then drag the cells' fill handle down the column to create the series.

Tip: The **fill handle** is the small black square in the lower-right corner of the selection. When you point to the fill handle, the pointer changes to a cross.

By Using Formulas

Formulas let you create dynamic time series: change the first time, and the others update automatically (AutoFill, in contrast, creates static series of literal times). To create a dynamic series, enter the starting time in a cell and then use formulas (copied down the column) to generate additional times in the series.

For example, to create a series of times with 15-minute intervals, enter the first time of the series in cell A1, enter

`=A1+TIME(0,15,0)`

in cell A2, and then copy this formula down the column as many times as needed.

See also "Generating a Series of Dates" on page 86.

Converting Text to Times

If you import times coded as text strings that TIMEVALUE can't convert, then you can use Excel's text functions to extract the hours, minutes, and seconds separately and then use TIME or TIMEVALUE to convert these time parts to a time serial number.

For example, military-time format is *hhmm*—a two-digit hour followed by a two-digit minute (0000–2359). If cell A1 contains the text value 1630 (representing 4:30 PM), then

`=TIMEVALUE(LEFT(A1,2) & ":" & RIGHT(A1,2))`

and

`=TIMEVALUE(TEXT(A1,"00\:00"))`

return 16:30:00 (serial number 0.6875). In the first formula, the text functions LEFT and RIGHT extract the digits of the hour and minute, respectively. In the second formula, the TEXT function returns a formatted string that TIMEVALUE can convert to a time.

If the time doesn't have leading zeros (0–2359), then use

`=TIMEVALUE(LEFT(TEXT(A1,"0000"),2) & ":" & RIGHT(A1,2))`

See also "Converting Text to Dates" on page 88.

Rounding Times

You can use the ROUND function to round a time to the nearest minute, hour, half hour, and so on.

ROUND(*number, num_digits*)

If *num_digits* is greater than 0 (zero), then *number* is rounded to the specified number of decimal places. If *num_digits* is 0, then *number* is rounded to the nearest integer. If *num_digits* is less than 0, then *number* is rounded to the left of the decimal point.

The following formula rounds the time in cell A1 to the nearest minute:

=ROUND(A1*1440,0)/1440

Multiplying the time by the number of minutes in a day (1440) yields the total minutes, which is rounded to a whole number (integer) and then converted back to a time by dividing by 1440. If cell A1 contains 10:18:35, then the result is 10:19:00.

Similarly, to round to the nearest hour:

=ROUND(A1*24,0)/24

The result is 10:00:00.

To round to the nearest half hour (30 minutes):

=ROUND(A1*24/0.5,0)*(0.5/24)

The result is 10:30:00.

To round to the nearest quarter hour (15 minutes):

=ROUND(A1*24/0.25,0)*(0.25/24)

The result is 10:15:00.

16 Getting Started with Sums & Counts

Summing and counting values are the most common spreadsheet operations, and Excel's capabilities go far beyond routine SUM and COUNT formulas. Part III (Chapters 16–21) of this book shows you how to use worksheet functions, array formulas, AutoSum, and other Excel features to summarize an entire range of values, or only values that meet specific conditions. If you're using an older version of Excel that doesn't support the latest worksheet functions, then you'll find equivalent formulas that work in Excel 2003 or earlier.

- Display sums and counts without using formulas.
- Master the basics of COUNT, COUNTA, COUNTBLANK, and other counting functions.
- Create conditional counts with COUNTIF and COUNTIFS.
- Calculate the mode for numeric or text values.
- Count unique values in a range.
- Count occurrences of specific text strings.
- Create frequency distributions and histograms.
- Master the basics of the SUM function.
- Use AutoSum to sum values quickly.
- Calculate running totals.

- Sum only the highest or lowest values in a range.
- Eliminate rounding errors in financial calculations.
- Sum every *n*th value in a range.
- Create conditional sums with SUMIF and SUMIFS.

Downloading the Sample Workbook

To follow along with or copy the examples in this book, download the Excel workbook excel_sums_counts.xlsx from *questingvolepress.com* (a .xls workbook is also included for pre-2007 versions of Excel). This workbook contains worksheets that demonstrate most of the example formulas.

Tip: If you're using Excel 2007 or later and sharing your workbooks with people using earlier versions of Excel, then read the Microsoft support article, "Save an Excel workbook for compatibility with earlier versions of Excel" at *support.office.com*.

Using the Example Formulas

When you adapt the example formulas in this book to use in your own Excel workbooks, keep the following issues in mind.

Named Ranges

Most of the example formulas use **named ranges** as function arguments: COUNT(data) or SUM(values), for example. When you use these formulas in your own worksheets, substitute either the actual range reference (A1:E8, for example) or a range name defined in your workbook (Formulas tab > Defined Names group > Name Manager).

If your data are in a table, then you can use table referencing in your formulas instead of creating named ranges. For example, if a table named Table1 has a column named Sales, then you can enter

```
=COUNTIFS(Table1[Sales],">=500",Table1[Sales],
"<=1000")
```

instead of manually creating a range named Sales and entering

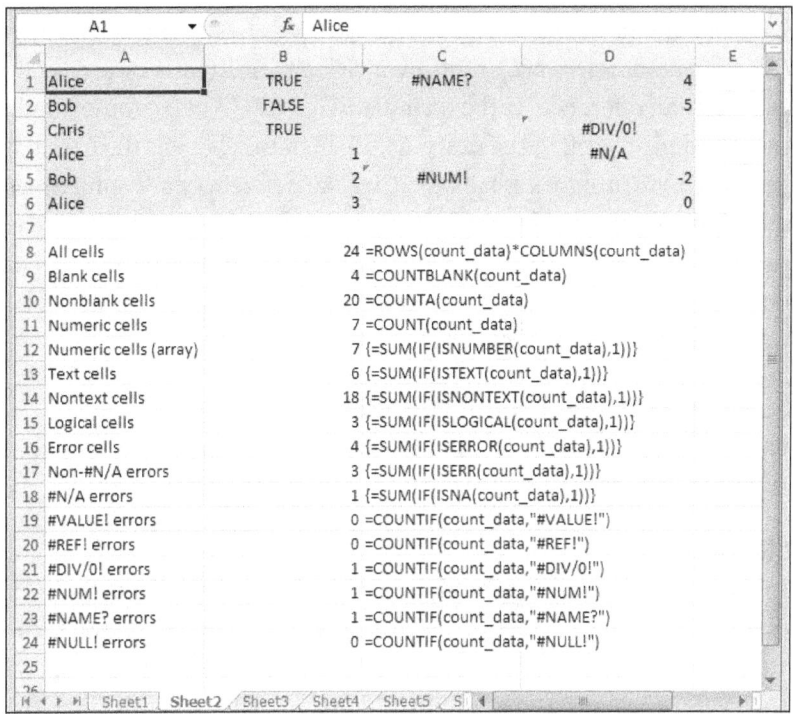

```
=COUNTIFS(Sales,">=500",Sales,"<=1000")
```

When you define a range as a table (Insert tab > Tables group > Table), Excel creates names automatically for the table and for each column in the table.

Array Formulas

A formula that's surrounded by braces { } is an **array formula**. For example,

```
{=SUM(IF(ISTEXT(values),1))}
```

Whenever you enter an array formula, you must press Ctrl+Shift+Enter (not just Enter). Don't type the braces manually; they will appear automatically in the formula bar. If you edit an existing array formula, then you must still press Ctrl+Shift+Enter; otherwise, the array formula will revert to a normal formula and return the wrong result. For details, read the Microsoft support article "Guidelines and examples of array formulas" at *support.office.com*.

Circular References

A formula that refers back to its own cell, either directly or indirectly, is a **circular reference**. If the formula =COUNT(A1:C3), for example, is entered in any cell in the range A1:C3, then Excel opens the Circular Reference Warning message box. Circular references are sometimes useful (notably in some financial and scientific calculations) and Excel can solve them iteratively, but they're most often unintentional. For details, read the Microsoft support article "Remove or allow a circular reference" at *support.office.com*.

Sums and Counts without Formulas

Excel offers a few ways to calculate counts and sums without using formulas.

Status Bar Display

In Excel 97 or later, a quick glance at the **status bar** shows the sum, count, and other calculations for the selected range. By default, the status bar (which runs along the bottom of the Excel window) displays the average, count, and sum of the selected cells. To customize the display, right-click the status bar to open the Customize Status Bar menu. To make the status bar show the number of nonempty cells in the selected range, select Count. To show the number of numeric cells in the selected range, select Numerical Count.

Tables

If your data are in a **table** (Insert tab > Tables group > Table), then you can use AutoFilter criteria to count or sum visible values. To filter (hide) unwanted rows, click ▼ in the table's Header row. To turn on a table's Total row, select any cell in the table and then choose Table Tools > Design tab > Table Style Options group > Total Row. For details, read the Microsoft support article "Overview of Excel tables" at *support.office.com*. (Tables were called **lists** in older versions of Excel.)

Tip: The special database functions DCOUNT, DCOUNTA, and DSUM also provide ways to count and sum values in a table.

	A	B	C	D	E	F
1	Tree	Height	Age	Yield	Profit	
2	Apple	18	20	14	105	
3	Pear	12	12	10	96	
4	Cherry	13	14	9	105	
5	Apple	14	15	10	75	
6	Pear	9	8	8	76.8	
7	Apple	8	9	6	45	
8	Total				502.8	

Formula bar: E8 = =SUBTOTAL(109,[Profit])

Dropdown options: None, Average, Count, Count Numbers, Max, Min, **Sum**, StdDev, Var, More Functions.

Pivot Tables

If your data are in a table or worksheet database, then you can create a **pivot table** (Insert tab > Tables group > PivotTable) to get sums, counts, and other calculations. Pivot tables are concise, flexible summaries of lists of values, and are one of Excel's most-powerful features. For details, read the Microsoft support article "Create a PivotTable to analyze worksheet data" at *support.office.com*.

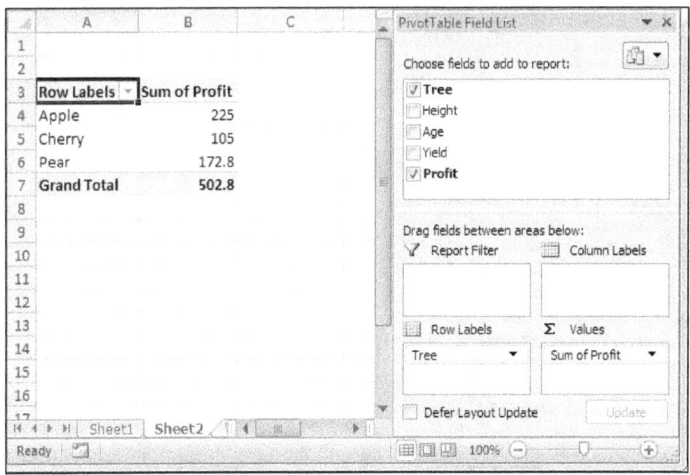

Chapter 16 Getting Started with Sums & Counts

17 Counting Basics

This chapter brings you up to speed with Excel's counting functions. If the built-in functions can't solve your problem, then often an array formula can help.

Counting Functions

You can use the following worksheet functions to create formulas that return the number of cells in a specified range that meet certain criteria.

COLUMNS(*array*)
>Counts the columns in a range. See "Counting All Cells in a Range (ROWS & COLUMNS)" on page 109.

COUNT(*value1*, [*value2*], …)
>Counts the numeric cells in a range. See "Counting Numeric Cells (COUNT)" on page 110.

COUNTA(*value1*, [*value2*], …)
>Counts the nonblank cells in a range. See "Counting Nonblank Cells (COUNTA)" on page 110.

COUNTBLANK(*range*)
>Counts the blank cells in a range. See "Counting Blank Cells (COUNTBLANK)" on page 109.

COUNTIF(*range*, *criteria*)
>Counts cells in a range based on a single criterion. See "Counting Cells Based on a Single Criterion (COUNTIF)" on page 113.

COUNTIFS(*criteria_range1, criteria1,* [*criteria_range2, criteria2*],...)
: Counts cells across multiple ranges based on multiple criteria. See "Counting Cells Based on Multiple Criteria (COUNTIFS)" on page 115.

Tip: COUNTIFS is available in Excel 2007 or later.

DCOUNT(*database, field, criteria*)
: Counts the numeric cells in a field (column) in a table (also called a list or worksheet database) that meet one or more given criteria.

DCOUNTA(*database, field, criteria*)
: Counts the nonblank cells in a field in a table that meet one or more given criteria.

FREQUENCY(*data_array, bins_array*)
: Returns a frequency distribution (how often values occur within a range of values) as a vertical array. See Chapter 19.

Tip: FREQUENCY returns an array and so must be entered as an array formula (page 103).

ROWS(*array*)
: Counts the rows in a range. See "Counting All Cells in a Range (ROWS & COLUMNS)" on page 109.

SUBTOTAL(*function_num, ref1,* [*ref2*],...)
: Counts cells that comprise a subtotal in a list. When *function_num* is 2, SUBTOTAL acts like the COUNT function. When *function_num* is 3, SUBTOTAL acts like the COUNTA function.

Basic Counting Formulas

Using the counting functions to create basic counting formulas is straightforward. The sample workbook has a worksheet that uses formulas in this section to summarize the contents of range A1:D6—a 24-cell range named *count_data*.

	A	B	C	D
1	Alice	TRUE	#NAME?	4
2	Bob	FALSE		5
3	Chris	TRUE		#DIV/0!
4	Alice		1	#N/A
5	Bob		2	#NUM!	-2
6	Alice		3	0
7				
8	All cells		24	=ROWS(count_data)*COLUMNS(count_data)
9	Blank cells		4	=COUNTBLANK(count_data)
10	Nonblank cells		20	=COUNTA(count_data)
11	Numeric cells		7	=COUNT(count_data)
12	Numeric cells (array)		7	{=SUM(IF(ISNUMBER(count_data),1))}
13	Text cells		6	{=SUM(IF(ISTEXT(count_data),1))}
14	Nontext cells		18	{=SUM(IF(ISNONTEXT(count_data),1))}
15	Logical cells		3	{=SUM(IF(ISLOGICAL(count_data),1))}
16	Error cells		4	{=SUM(IF(ISERROR(count_data),1))}
17	Non-#N/A errors		3	{=SUM(IF(ISERR(count_data),1))}
18	#N/A errors		1	{=SUM(IF(ISNA(count_data),1))}
19	#VALUE! errors		0	=COUNTIF(count_data,"#VALUE!")
20	#REF! errors		0	=COUNTIF(count_data,"#REF!")
21	#DIV/0! errors		1	=COUNTIF(count_data,"#DIV/0!")
22	#NUM! errors		1	=COUNTIF(count_data,"#NUM!")
23	#NAME? errors		1	=COUNTIF(count_data,"#NAME?")
24	#NULL! errors		0	=COUNTIF(count_data,"#NULL!")

Counting All Cells in a Range (ROWS & COLUMNS)

Excel lacks a function that simply counts cells in a range. To count the total number of cells in a range (blank and nonblank cells), multiply the return values from the ROWS and COLUMNS functions. The following formula returns the number of cells in a range named *count_data*:

=ROWS(count_data)*COLUMNS(count_data)

Counting Blank Cells (COUNTBLANK)

The following formula returns the number of blank cells in the range named *count_data*:

=COUNTBLANK(count_data)

A blank cell isn't the same as an empty cell, though you'll often see these terms used equivalently. An **empty cell** contains nothing; all cells in a newly created blank workbook are empty cells, for example. A **blank cell**, on the other hand, may contain nothing (like an empty cell) or it may contain a formula that returns an **empty string** (""). Cells that contain empty strings are counted by COUNTBLANK. For testing purposes, you can quickly enter an empty string by typing the formula ="". To return an empty string in a cell based on, say, whether the value in cell A1 is greater than 100, type the formula =IF(A1>100,"",A1).

Tip: A cell that contains an invisible zero value is not blank, and so isn't counted by COUNTBLANK. To toggle the visibility of zeros, choose File tab > Options > Advanced category > "Display options for this worksheet" section > "Show a zero in cells that have zero value".

To count blanks in entire columns, specify the starting and ending column letters, separated by a colon (:). To count the blank cells in column A, for example, type

=COUNTBLANK(A:A)

To count blanks in entire rows, specify the starting and ending row numbers, separated by a colon (:). To count the blank cells in rows 5 through 10, for example, type

=COUNTBLANK(5:10)

To count blank cells in a specific worksheet, type the worksheet name, followed by an exclamation point (!), followed by a range. To count the blank cells in the range named *count_data* in the worksheet named *Sheet2*, for example, type

=COUNTBLANK(Sheet2!count_data)

Counting Nonblank Cells (COUNTA)

Nonblank cells include cells that contain values, text, logical values (TRUE or FALSE), or empty strings. The following formula returns the number of nonblank cells in the range named *count_data*:

=COUNTA(count_data)

Counting Numeric Cells (COUNT)

Numeric cells are cells that contain numbers, including dates or times (which Excel stores internally as serial numbers). The following formula returns the number of numeric cells in the range named *count_data*:

```
=COUNT(count_data)
```

The equivalent array formula uses Excel's ISNUMBER function, which returns TRUE if its argument refers to any numeric cell:

```
{=SUM(IF(ISNUMBER(count_data),1))}
```

Counting Nontext Cells

To count nontext cells, use Excel's ISNONTEXT function, which returns TRUE if its argument refers to any nontext cell, including empty cells. The following array formula returns the number of nontext cells in the range named *count_data*:

```
{=SUM(IF(ISNONTEXT(count_data),1))}
```

Counting Text Cells

To count text cells, use Excel's ISTEXT function, which returns TRUE if its argument refers to any text cell, including cells that contain empty strings. The following array formula returns the number of text cells in the range named *count_data*:

```
{=SUM(IF(ISTEXT(count_data),1))}
```

Counting Logical Values

To count logical values (TRUE or FALSE), use Excel's ISLOGICAL function, which returns TRUE if its argument refers to any logical value. The following array formula returns the number of logical values in the range named *count_data*:

```
{=SUM(IF(ISLOGICAL(count_data),1))}
```

Counting Error Values

To determine whether a cell contains an error value, you can use the following functions:

- ISERROR(*value*) returns TRUE if its argument refers to any error value (#N/A, #VALUE!, #REF!, #DIV/0!, #NUM!, #NAME?, or #NULL!).

- ISERR(*value*) returns TRUE if its argument refers to any error value except #N/A.

- ISNA(*value*) returns TRUE if its argument refers to the error value #N/A.

Tip: The error value #N/A (meaning "value not available") differs from the other error values in that #N/A generally isn't a "real" error. Rather, #N/A is used as a placeholder to mark missing information, avoiding the problem of unintentionally including empty cells in calculations—which Excel might interpret as zeros or empty strings. (When a formula refers to a cell containing #N/A, the formula returns the #N/A error value.) To enter the #N/A error value in a cell, type *#N/A* directly or use the NA function: =NA().

The following array formula returns the number of error values in the range named *count_data*:

```
{=SUM(IF(ISERROR(count_data),1))}
```

Similarly, you can use ISERR or ISNA in place of ISERROR.

To count specific types of errors, use the COUNTIF function with the name of the error as criteria. The following formula, for example, counts the number of #NAME? error values in the range named count_data:

```
=COUNTIF(count_data,"#NAME?")
```

18 Counting Tricks

Advanced counting formulas let you count cells that meet complex selection criteria. The sample workbook has worksheets that use the formulas in this chapter.

Counting Cells Based on a Single Criterion (COUNTIF)

The COUNTIF function counts cells in a range that meet a single criterion:

> COUNTIF(*range, criteria*)

where

> *range* (required) is the range of one or more cells to count, including numbers or names, arrays, or references that contain numbers. Blank and text values are ignored.
>
> *criteria* (required) is a number, expression, cell reference, text string, or function that determines which cells will be counted. For example, *criteria* can be expressed as 25, "25", ">25", "widgets", B4, or TODAY(). Any text criteria or any criteria that include logical or mathematical symbols must be enclosed in double quotes ("). If *criteria* is numeric, then double quotes aren't required. You can use the wildcard characters, question mark (?) and asterisk (*), in *criteria*. A question mark matches any single character; an asterisk matches any sequence of characters. To find an actual question mark or asterisk, type a tilde (~) before the character.

The following examples show several ways to use COUNTIF in formulas. These formulas all work with a range named *range*.

=COUNTIF(range,10)
   Counts cells containing the value 10.

=COUNTIF(range,">10")
   Counts cells greater than 10.

=COUNTIF(range,"<0")
   Counts cells containing a negative value.

=COUNTIF(range,"<>0")
   Counts cells not equal to 0.

=COUNTIF(range,"<"&AVERAGE(range))
   Counts cells with a value less than the average.

=COUNTIF(range,">"&AVERAGE(range)+STDEV(range)*2)
   Counts cells with a value greater than two standard deviations above the mean.

=COUNTIF(range,1)+COUNTIF(range,-1)
   Counts cells containing the value 1 or –1.

=COUNTIF(range,A1)
   Counts cells equal to the contents of cell A1.

=COUNTIF(range,"<="&A1)
   Counts cells less than or equal to the value in cell A1.

=COUNTIF(range,"*")
   Counts cells containing text.

=COUNTIF(range,"?????")
   Counts text cells containing exactly five characters.

=COUNTIF(range,"Jane")
   Counts cells containing only the single word *Jane* (case-insensitive).

=COUNTIF(range,"*Smith*")
   Counts cells containing the text *Smith* anywhere within the text (case-insensitive).

=COUNTIF(range,"A*")
: Counts cells containing text that starts with the letter *A* (case-insensitive).

=COUNTIF(range,TODAY())
: Counts cells containing the current date.

=COUNTIF(range,TRUE)
: Counts cells containing the logical value TRUE.

=COUNTIF(range,TRUE)+COUNTIF(range,FALSE)
: Counts cells containing a logical value (TRUE or FALSE).

=COUNTIF(range,"#N/A")
: Returns the number of cells containing the error value #N/A.

=COUNTIF(range,"#DIV/0!")
: Returns the number of cells containing the error value #DIV/0!.

Counting Cells Based on Multiple Criteria (COUNTIFS)

The COUNTIFS function counts cells across multiple ranges based on multiple criteria:

COUNTIFS(*criteria_range1, criteria1,* [*criteria_range2, criteria2*]...)

where

criteria_range1 (required) is the first range of cells in which to evaluate the associated criteria.

criteria1 (required) is a number, expression, cell reference, text string, or function that determines which cells will be counted. For example, *criteria* can be expressed as 25, "25", ">25", "widgets", B4, or TODAY(). Any text criteria or any criteria that include logical or mathematical symbols must be enclosed in then double quotes ("). If *criteria* is numeric, then double quotes aren't required. You can use the wildcard characters, question mark (?) and asterisk (*), in *criteria*. A question mark matches any single character; an asterisk matches any sequence of characters. To find an actual question mark or asterisk, type a tilde (~) before the character.

criteria_range2, criteria2,... (optional) are additional ranges and their associated criteria. Each additional range must have the same number of rows and columns as *criteria_range1*. The ranges don't have to be adjacent to each other. Up to 127 range–criteria pairs are allowed.

Tip: COUNTIFS is available in Excel 2007 or later.

Using AND Logic for Counts

Use AND logic in formulas to count cells that meet *all* specified criteria. The following formula counts cells in the range named *sales* that contain a value greater or equal to 500 and less than or equal to 1000:

```
=COUNTIFS(sales,">=500",sales,"<=1000")
```

Tip: If the criteria argument is a reference to an empty cell, then COUNTIFS treats the empty cell as a 0 value.

In Excel 2003 or earlier, use the following equivalent COUNTIF formula.

```
=COUNTIF(sales,">=500")-COUNTIF(sales,">1000")
```

The preceding formula counts the number of values that are greater than or equal to 500 and then subtracts the number of values that are greater than 1000. Note that the criterion in the formula's second COUNTIF function is ">1000", and not ">=1000"; using the latter criterion would subtract any sales values equal to 1000, which isn't equivalent to the original COUNTIFS formula. If changing the criteria in this way is confusing, then you can use the following straightforward array formula instead:

```
{=SUM((sales>=500)*(sales<=1000))}
```

	A	B	C	D
1	year	country	region	sales
2	2012	US	East	440
3	2012	US	West	1130
4	2012	US	North	220
5	2012	US	South	750
6	2013	US	East	360
7	2013	US	West	1410
8	2013	US	North	220
9	2013	US	South	540
10	2012	Canada	East	1430
11	2012	Canada	West	620
12	2012	Canada	North	1470
13	2012	Canada	South	810
14	2013	Canada	East	750
15	2013	Canada	West	1230
16	2013	Canada	North	1470
17	2013	Canada	South	1350
18	2012	Mexico	East	970
19	2012	Mexico	West	1000
20	2012	Mexico	North	610
21	2012	Mexico	South	240
22	2013	Mexico	East	1460
23	2013	Mexico	West	740
24	2013	Mexico	North	750
25	2013	Mexico	South	810
26				
27	**Using AND Logic for Counts**			
28	11 Count sales between 500 and 1000 (COUNTIFS; Excel 2007 or later)			
29	11 Count sales between 500 and 1000 (COUNTIF)			
30	11 Count sales between 500 and 1000 (array formula)			
31	3 Count 2013 Canada sales >= 1000 (COUNTIFS; Excel 2007 or later)			
32	3 Count 2013 Canada sales >= 1000 (SUMPRODUCT)			
33	3 Count 2013 Canada sales >= 1000 (array formula)			
34				
35	**Using OR Logic for Counts**			
36	16 Count sales in the US or Canada (COUNTIF)			
37	16 Count sales in the US or Canada (array formula)			
38	19 Count sales in 2013 or in the US or >= 1000 (array formula)			
39				
40	**Mixing AND and OR Logic for Counts**			
41	8 Count 2013 sales in the US or Canada (COUNTIFS; Excel 2007 or later)			
42	8 Count 2013 sales in the US or Canada (array formula)			

COUNTIFS also lets you specify criteria based on cells in multiple ranges. For example, to count items that meet the criteria

(year is 2013) AND (country is Canada) AND (sales >= 1000)

use the following formula:

```
=COUNTIFS(year,2013,country,"Canada",sales,">=1000")
```

The preceding formula uses three range–criteria pairs as arguments. COUNTIFS applies each range's criteria one cell at a time. If all of the first cells meet their associated criteria, then the count increases by 1. If all of the second cells meet their associated criteria, then the count increases by 1 again, and so on until all the cells are evaluated.

In Excel 2003 or earlier, use the following equivalent SUMPRODUCT formula:

```
=SUMPRODUCT((year=2013)*(country="Canada")*
(sales>=1000))
```

Or use this array formula:

```
{=SUM((year=2013)*(country="Canada")*(sales>=1000))}
```

Using OR Logic for Counts

Use OR logic in formulas to count cells that meet *any* specified criteria. If the criteria all apply to the same range, then you can use multiple COUNTIF functions to sum nonoverlapping counts. The following formula counts sales made in the US or Canada:

```
=COUNTIF(country,"US")+COUNTIF(country,"Canada")
```

The equivalent array formula is:

```
{=SUM(COUNTIF(country,{"US","Canada"}))}
```

If the criteria span multiple ranges, then you can't use the preceding formulas because they double-count cells that meet more than one of the criteria. To solve this problem, use an array formula instead of COUNTIF. For example, to count items that meet the criteria

(year is 2013) OR (country is US) OR (sales >= 1000)

use the following array formula:

```
{=SUM(IF((year=2013)+(country="US")+
(sales>=1000),1))}
```

Mixing AND and OR Logic for Counts

Summing multiple COUNTIFS functions lets you combine AND and OR logic in a single formula. For example, to count items that meet the criteria

> (year is 2013) AND ((country is US) OR (country is Canada))

use the following formula:

```
=COUNTIFS(year,2013,country,"US")+
COUNTIFS(year,2013,country,"Canada")
```

The preceding formula requires repeating the AND criteria in every COUNTIFS function, which is unwieldy for formulas that involve many criteria. A more-concise array formula (also for use in Excel 2003 or earlier) is:

```
{=SUM((year=2013)*((country="US")+
(country="Canada")))}
```

Counting the Most Frequently Occurring Value (Mode)

The MODE function returns the most frequently occurring value in a range, called the **mode**. The following formula returns the mode of the range named *dice_rolls*:

```
=MODE(dice_rolls)
```

The **frequency** of the mode is the number of times that it appears in the range:

```
=COUNTIF(dice_rolls,MODE(dice_rolls))
```

MODE returns the #N/A error value if the range contains no duplicate values.

Tip: If more than one most-frequent value exists, then the formulas in this section return only the first in the range. In Excel 2013 or later, use MODE.MULT (to return multiple modes) or MODE.SNGL (to return a single mode) instead of MODE.

	A	B	C	D
1	dice_rolls		names	
2	8		Bob	
3	11		Bob	
4	7		Alice	
5	8		Chris	
6	5		Chris	
7	7		Alice	
8	12		Chris	
9	7		Chris	
10	6		Alice	
11	6		Bob	
12	9		Bob	
13	5		Bob	
14	7		Alice	
15	7		Alice	
16	8		Bob	
17	3		Bob	
18	11		Bob	
19	7		Bob	
20	8		Bob	
21	3		Chris	
22				
23	7	Mode (numeric only)	Bob	Mode (text or values)
24	7	Mode (text or values)	10	Mode frequency (text or values)
25	6	Mode frequency (numeric only)		

The MODE function works for only numeric values, ignoring empty cells and cells that contain text or logical values. To find the most frequently occurring (case-insensitive) text entry in the range named *names*, use the following array formula:

={INDEX(names,MATCH(MAX(COUNTIF(names,names)),
COUNTIF(names,names),0))}

The frequency of the mode (text or values) is the array formula:

{=MAX(COUNTIF(names,names))}

Counting Unique Values

The following array formula returns the number of unique values in the range named *eruptions*:

```
{=SUM(1/COUNTIF(eruptions,eruptions))}
```

You can add an IF condition to handle blank cells or other types of values:

```
{=SUM(IF(COUNTIF(eruptions,eruptions)=0,"",
1/COUNTIF(eruptions,eruptions)))}
```

	A	B	C	D
1	eruptions			
2	0			
3	0			
4	0			
5	0			
6	1			
7	1			
8	1			
9	1			
10	1			
11	2			
12	4			
13	4			
14	5			
15				
16		5	Unique values	
17		5	Unique values (IF condition)	

Tip: Comprehending these formulas requires an understanding of array formulas. To see how the first formula works, break it into subformulas: enter the array formula {=COUNTIF(eruptions,eruptions)} in a range that's the same size as *eruptions*, say G2:G14. Next, enter the array formula {=1/G2:G14} in H2:H14. The sum of the values in H2:H14 is the number of unique values.

Counting Text Strings

This section shows you how to count occurrences of a text string (one or more characters) in a range of cells. In the following example formulas, the range of cells to search is named *strings* and the cell containing the text to search for is named *find_text*.

	A	B	C
1	strings	find_text	
2	Alice	bob	
3	Bob		
4	Chris		
5	alice		
6	bob		
7	chris		
8	al		
9	bo		
10	ch		
11	Alice Bob Chris		
12	alice bob chris		
13	BobBobBob		
14	bobbobbob		
15			
16	Entire Contents of Cells		
17		2	Case-insensitive
18		1	Case-sensitive
19			
20	Partial Contents of Cells		
21		6	Case-insensitive
22		6	Case-insensitive (SEARCH)
23		3	Case-sensitive
24		3	Case-sensitive (FIND)
25			
26	Frequency of Strings		
27		10	Case-insensitive
28		5	Case-sensitive

Entire Contents of Cells

The following formulas count matches only when the entire contents of a cell in *strings* matches the contents of the cell *find_text*.

The following case-insensitive formula uses the COUNTIF function to count matching cells:

```
=COUNTIF(strings,find_text)
```

The case-sensitive version is the following array formula:

```
{=SUM(IF(EXACT(strings,find_text),1))}
```

Partial Contents of Cells

The following formulas count matches when the partial (or entire) contents of a cell in *strings* matches the contents of the cell *find_text*.

The following case-insensitive formula uses the COUNTIF function and wildcard characters to count matching cells:

```
=COUNTIF(strings,"*"&find_text&"*")
```

An equivalent array formula that uses the SEARCH function is:

```
{=SUM(IF(NOT(ISERROR(SEARCH(find_text,strings))),
1))}
```

The ISERROR function is needed because SEARCH returns an error value if *find_text* isn't found in *strings*.

The case-sensitive equivalents of the two preceding formulas are the array formulas:

```
{=SUM(IF(LEN(strings)-LEN(SUBSTITUTE(strings,
find_text,""))>0,1))}
```

and

```
{=SUM(IF(NOT(ISERROR(FIND(find_text,strings))),1))}
```

Like SEARCH, the FIND function returns an error if *find_text* isn't found in *strings*. Unlike SEARCH, the FIND function is case-sensitive.

Frequency of Strings

The following formulas count the total number of times that the contents of the cell *find_text* occurs in the cells in *strings* (*find_text* can occur more than once in a single cell).

The following case-insensitive array formula counts the total number of occurrences of *find_text* in strings:

```
{=(SUM(LEN(strings))-SUM(LEN(SUBSTITUTE(UPPER(
strings),UPPER(find_text),""))))/LEN(find_text)}
```

The case-sensitive version is:

```
{=(SUM(LEN(strings))-SUM(LEN(SUBSTITUTE(strings,
find_text,""))))/LEN(find_text)}
```

19 Frequency Distributions

A frequency distribution is a summary table that shows the number of occurrences of each value in a range. Excel offers a few ways to create frequency distributions:

- The FREQUENCY function
- Custom formulas
- The Analysis ToolPak add-in
- A pivot table

Each example in this chapter uses the same data to create a frequency distribution of student grades, showing the counts of As, Bs, Cs, and so on. The range of cells named *score* contains 30 test scores. To build a frequency distribution, students are assigned letter grades (A–F) based on their test scores (0–100).

Using the FREQUENCY Function

Excel's FREQUENCY function calculates how often values occur within a range of values, and then returns a vertical array of frequency counts. Because FREQUENCY returns an array, it must be entered as an array formula (page 103) in a multicell range. FREQUENCY ignores blank cells and text. The syntax of FREQUENCY is:

FREQUENCY(*data_array, bins_array*)

where

data_array (required) is an array of or reference to a set of values for which you want to count frequencies. If *data_array* contains no values, then FREQUENCY returns an array of zeros.

bins_array (required) is an array of or reference to intervals into which you want to group the values in *data_array*. If *bins_array* contains no values, then FREQUENCY returns the number of elements in *data_array*.

The sample workbook has a worksheet that contains test scores for 30 students in cells B2:B31. The range is named *score*. The range C2:C6, named *bins*, contains the bins used for the frequency distribution. Each cell in this bin range contains the upper limit for the bin. Here, the bins are ≤59 (F), 60–69 (D), 70–79 (C), 80–89 (B), and 90–100 (A).

Tip: To use fractional numbers instead of integers as grade cutoff points, change the upper bin limits from 59 to 59.99, 69 to 69.99, and so on.

To create a frequency distribution, select a range of cells that's the same size as the bin range (here, 5R × 1C) and then enter the following array formula:

```
{=FREQUENCY(score,bins)}
```

The array formula returns the count of values in the score range that fall into each bin.

Tip: FREQUENCY actually returns an array that contains one more element than the number of elements in the bins array. This extra element contains the count of any values greater than the highest bin interval. In this example, FREQUENCY is entered into five cells rather than six cells because no score exceeds 100, so the last returned element (which contains zero) is unnecessary.

To create a frequency distribution of percentages, use the array formula:

```
{=FREQUENCY(score,bins)/COUNT(score)}
```

You can chart a frequency distribution as a histogram (column chart).

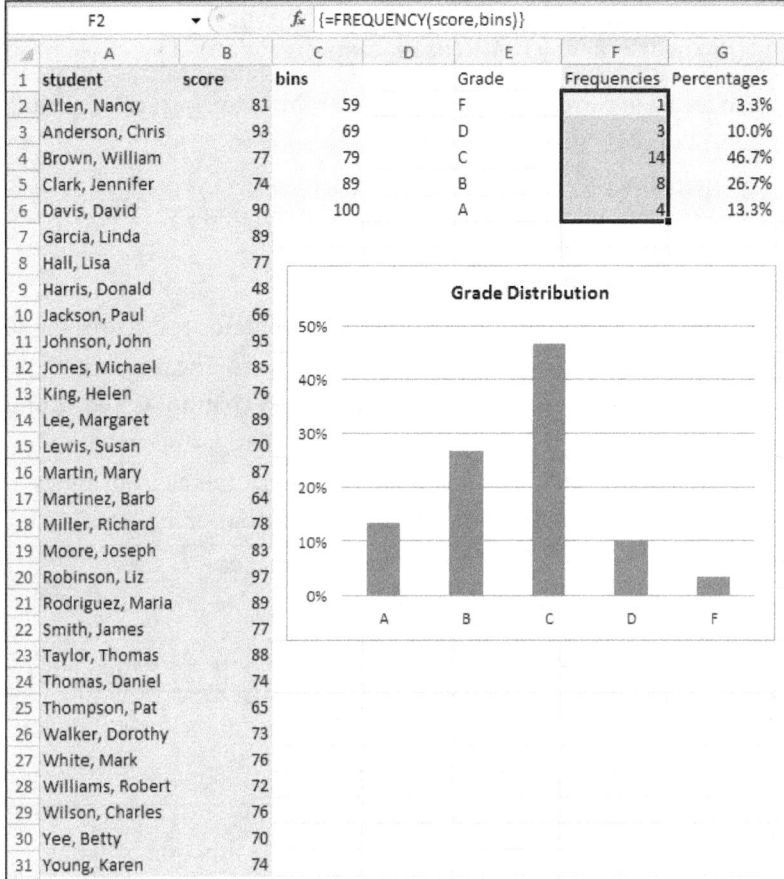

Creating Evenly Spaced Bins

Rather than creating bin endpoints manually, you can enter the following array formula in an $n \times 1$ (vertical) array to create n evenly spaced bins for the values in the range named *data_array*:

```
{=MIN(data_array)+(ROW(INDIRECT("1:n"))*
(MAX(data_array)-MIN(data_array)+1)/n)-1}
```

This array formula creates n bins, based on the values in the *data_array* (n is a positive integer). The highest bin value equals the maximum value in the range.

To create ten evenly spaced bins, for example, enter the following array formula in a 10 × 1 range:

```
{=MIN(data_array)+(ROW(INDIRECT("1:10")))*
(MAX(data_array)-MIN(data_array)+1)/10)-1}
```

To create five evenly spaced bins, enter the following array formula in a 5 × 1 range:

```
{=MIN(data_array)+(ROW(INDIRECT("1:5")))*
(MAX(data_array)-MIN(data_array)+1)/5)-1}
```

Using Custom Formulas

The sample workbook has a worksheet that contains test scores for 30 students in cells B2:B31. The range is named *score*. The minimum and maximum values for each letter grade appear in columns C and D, and column E contains the corresponding letter grades. A student with a test score between 70 and 79 (inclusive), for example, gets a C. Formulas in columns F and G calculate the frequency distribution of letter grades.

	F35			f_x	=COUNTIFS(score,">="&C35,score,"<="&D35)	
	A	B	C	D	E	F	G
33			Using Custom Formulas				
34			Min score	Max score	Grade	Frequencies	Percentages
35			90	100	A	4	13.3%
36			80	89	B	8	26.7%
37			70	79	C	14	46.7%
38			60	69	D	3	10.0%
39			0	59	F	1	3.3%

The formula in cell F35 uses the COUNTIFS function to count the number of scores that get an A:

```
=COUNTIFS(score,">="&C35,score,"<="&D35)
```

This formula was copied to the four cells below F35.

In Excel 2003 or earlier, use the following equivalent single-cell array formula (also copied to the four cells below F35):

```
{=SUM((score>=C35)*(score<=D35))}
```

The formulas in column G calculate the percentage of scores for each letter grade. The formula in G35 (which was copied to the four cells below G35) is:

```
=F35/SUM($F$35:$F$39)
```

Using the Analysis ToolPak

Excel's Analysis ToolPak add-in provides tools for doing statistical and engineering analyses. After you load the Analysis ToolPak, you can use the Histogram option to create a frequency distribution.

To load the Analysis ToolPak (Excel 2007 or later):

1. Choose File tab > Options > Add-Ins category.
2. In the Manage box, select Excel Add-ins and then click Go.
3. In the "Add-Ins available" box, select the Analysis ToolPak checkbox, and then click OK.

   If Analysis ToolPak isn't listed in the "Add-Ins available" box, then click Browse to find it.

4. If you're prompted that the Analysis ToolPak isn't currently installed on your computer, then click Yes to install it.

   When you load the Analysis ToolPak, the Data Analysis command is added to the Analysis group on the Data tab.

To load the Analysis ToolPak (Excel 2003 or earlier):

1. Choose Tools > Add-Ins.
2. In the "Add-Ins available" box, select the Analysis ToolPak checkbox, and then click OK.

   If Analysis ToolPak isn't listed in the "Add-Ins available" box, then click Browse to find it.

3. If you're prompted that the Analysis ToolPak isn't currently installed on your computer, then click Yes to install it.

   When you load the Analysis ToolPak, the Data Analysis command is added to the Tools menu.

Tip: In the Add-Ins dialog box, the add-in Analysis ToolPak - VBA is also available. This add-in is for programmers, and you don't need to install it.

The sample workbook has a worksheet that contains test scores for 30 students in cells B2:B31. The range is named *score*. The range C2:C6, named *bins*, contains the bins used for the frequency distribution.

To create a frequency distribution by using the Analysis ToolPak:

1. In Excel 2007 or later, choose Data tab > Analysis group > Data Analysis.

   or

   In Excel 2003 or earlier, choose Tools > Data Analysis.

   The Data Analysis dialog box opens.

   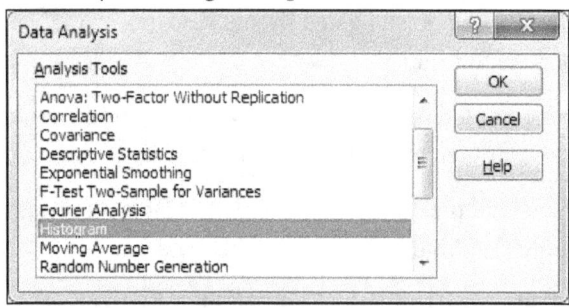

2. Select Histogram and then click OK.

   The Histogram dialog box opens.

   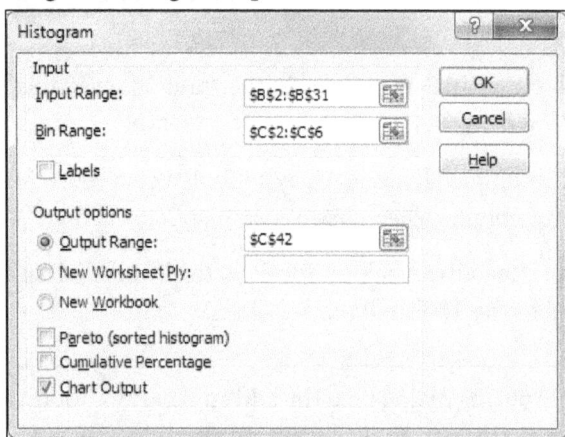

3. Specify the ranges for the data (Input Range), bins (Bin Range), and results (Output Range), select any additional options (such as Chart Output for a histogram), and then click OK.

The frequency distribution and selected options appear.

Tip: The frequency counts are constant values, not formulas. If you change the input data, then rerun Histogram to update the results.

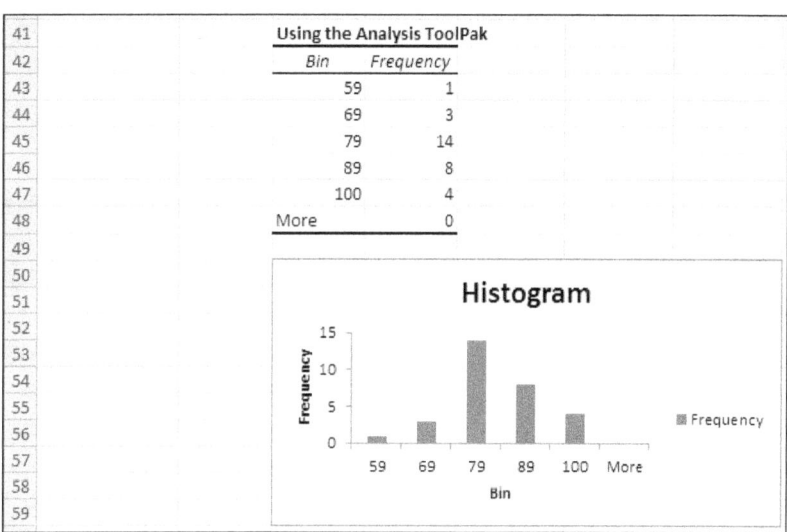

Chapter 19   Frequency Distributions   131

Using a Pivot Table

If your data are in a table (Insert tab > Tables group > Table), then you can use a pivot table (Insert tab > Tables group > PivotTable) to create a frequency distribution and a pivot chart to create a histogram. Pivot tables are concise, flexible summaries of lists of values, and are one of Excel's most-powerful features. For details, read the Microsoft support article "Create a PivotTable to analyze worksheet data" at *support.office.com*.

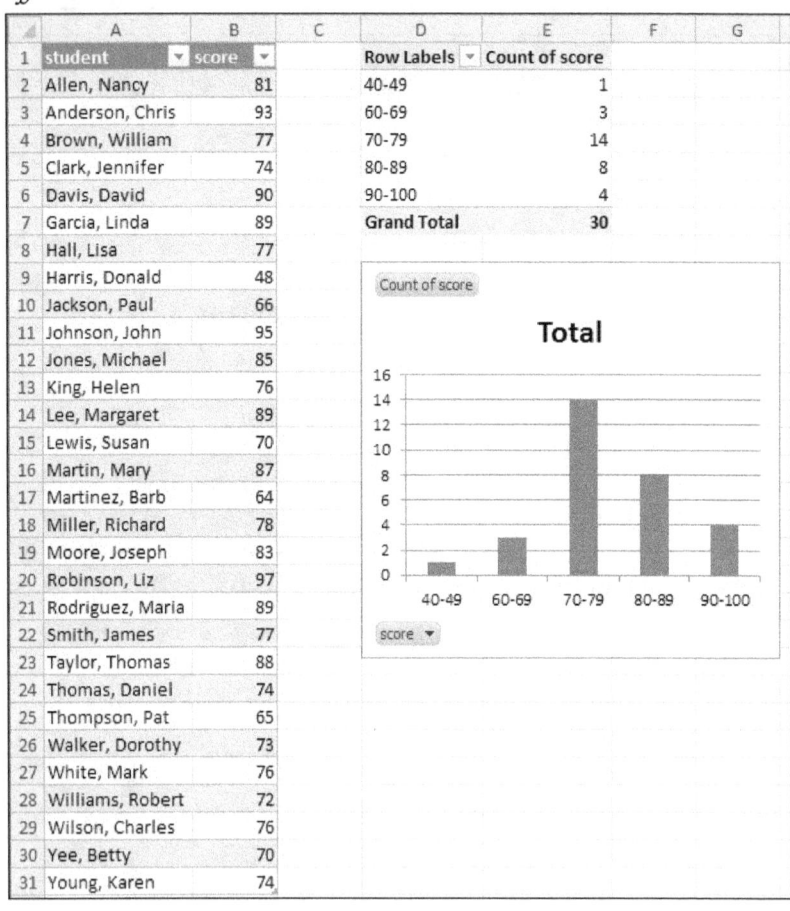

20 Summing Basics

This chapter brings you up to speed with Excel's summing functions. If the built-in functions can't solve your problem, then often an array formula (page 103) can help.

Summing Functions

You can use the following worksheet functions to create formulas that return the sum of cells in a specified range that meet certain criteria.

DSUM(*database, field, criteria*)
    Sums the numeric cells in a field (column) in a table (also called a list or worksheet database) that meet one or more given criteria.

SUBTOTAL(*function_num, ref1, [ref2], ...*)
    Sums cells that comprise a subtotal in a list. When *function_num* is 9, SUBTOTAL acts like the SUM function.

SUM(*number1, [number2], ...*)
    Sums its numeric arguments (page 134).

SUMIF(*range, criteria, [sum_range]*)
    Sums cells in a range based on a single criterion. See "Summing Values Based on a Single Criterion (SUMIF)" on page 144.

SUMIFS(*sum_range, criteria_range1, criteria1, [criteria_range2, criteria2], ...*)
    Sums cells in a range based on multiple criteria. See "Summing Values Based on Multiple Criteria (SUMIFS)" on page 147.

Tip: SUMIFS is available in Excel 2007 or later.

SUMPRODUCT(*array1*, [*array2*], [*array3*],...)
  Multiplies corresponding cells in two or more ranges, and returns the sum of those products.

Tip: Excel also includes summing functions that are used mainly for statistical formulas: DEVSQ, SUMSQ, SUMX2MY2, SUMX2PY2, and SUMXMY2. The SERIESSUM function returns the sum of a power series.

Basic Summing Formulas

The SUM function returns the sum of its arguments. In Excel 2007 or later, SUM accepts up to 255 arguments. In Excel 2003 or earlier, SUM accepts up to 30 arguments. The following types of arguments are valid:

- A single-cell reference: B5.
- A range reference: A1:B4.
- A constant number: 42.
- A string that can be converted to a number: "5".

Tip: SUM ignores strings in referenced cells (always treating them as 0), but when a string that can be converted to a number is used directly as an argument, SUM adds it to the result. If the two cells A1:A2 contain the strings "1" and "2", for example, then =SUM(A1:A2) returns 0, whereas =SUM("1", "2") returns 3.

- A logical value: TRUE or FALSE.

Tip: SUM is inconsistent in summing logical values. Logical values in referenced cells are always treated as 0, but when constant logical values are used as arguments, TRUE is treated as 1 and FALSE is treated as 0. If the four cells A1:A4 contain TRUE, FALSE, FALSE, TRUE, for example, then =SUM(A1:A4) returns 0, whereas =SUM(TRUE, FALSE, FALSE, TRUE) returns 2.

- An expression that returns a number: SQRT(ABS(-9)).
- An array constant: {1, 2, 3}.

Using the SUM function to create basic summing formulas is straightforward. The following formula returns the sum of all values in the range named *sum_data*:

```
=SUM(sum_data)
```

The following formula sums the values in noncontiguous ranges:

```
=SUM(A1:A4,B1:B4,C1:G1)
```

SUM treats each of its arguments independently and so double-counts values in overlapping ranges. If the six cells A1:A6 contain the values 1, 2, 3, 4, 5, and 6, for example, then

```
=SUM(A1:A6)
```

returns 21, and

```
=SUM(A1:A4,A3:A6)
```

returns 28 because cells A3 (3) and A4 (4) are summed twice.

To sum values in entire columns, specify the starting and ending column letters, separated by a colon (:). To sum cells in column A, for example, type

```
=SUM(A:A)
```

To sum values in entire rows, specify the starting and ending row numbers, separated by a colon (:). To sum values in rows 5 through 10, for example, type

```
=SUM(5:10)
```

To sum values in a specific worksheet, type the worksheet name, followed by an exclamation point (!), followed by a range. To sum values in the range named *sum_data* in the worksheet named *Sheet2*, for example, type

```
=SUM(Sheet2!sum_data)
```

You can mix argument types in SUM:

```
=SUM(B5,A1:B4,42,"5",TRUE,FALSE,
SQRT(ABS(-9)),{1,2,3})
```

Tip: SUM ignores missing arguments. The formula =SUM(1,,2,,3) has five arguments, two of which are missing.

Ignoring Errors in Sums

SUM returns an error value if any value in the summed range contains an error value (#N/A, #DIV/0!, #NAME?, and so on). If the cell A1 displays #N/A, for example, then =SUM(A1:A5) will return #N/A. (If the summed range contains a mix of error values, then SUM returns the first one that it encounters.)

To sum the values in the range named sum_data, ignoring any error values, use the following array formula:

```
{=SUM(IF(ISERROR(sum_data),"",sum_data))}
```

In Excel 2010 or later, you can use the AGGREGATE function to ignore errors when summing:

```
=AGGREGATE(9,6,sum_data)
```

The first argument (9) specifies SUM. The second argument (6) means ignore error values.

Using AutoSum

You can use **AutoSum** to quickly sum a range of numbers in a column or row.

To quickly sum a row or column of numbers in a range:

1. Select an empty cell below a column of numbers or to the right of a row of numbers.
2. Click the AutoSum (Σ) button, located in Home tab > Editing group and in Formulas tab > Function Library group. Keyboard shortcut: Alt+=.

   Excel selects what it determines to be the most likely range of data.

	A	B	C	D	E	F	G
1		Sales Q1	Sales Q2	Sales Q3	Sales Q4		
2	East	30	30	40	10	=SUM(B2:E2)	
3	West	40	20	50	30		
4	North	40	10	30	20		
5	South	40	20	50	50		
6							

3. Click AutoSum again (or press Enter) to accept the proposed range, or select your own range and then click AutoSum again (or press Enter). To cancel AutoSum, press Esc.

AutoSum includes the following features:

- To insert a function other than SUM, click the small arrow on the AutoSum button. You can choose AVERAGE, COUNT, MAX, or MIN, or choose More Functions to open the Insert Function dialog box.

- To enter similar SUM formulas in a range of cells, select the entire range and then click the AutoSum button. Excel inserts a formula in each of the selected cells. To create row sums for the range B2:E5, for example, select the range F2:F5 and then click the AutoSum button.

	A	B	C	D	E	F
1		Sales Q1	Sales Q2	Sales Q3	Sales Q4	
2	East	30	30	40	10	
3	West	40	20	50	30	
4	North	40	10	30	20	
5	South	40	20	50	50	
6						

- To sum both across and down a table of numbers, select the range of numbers plus an extra column to the right and an extra row at the bottom. Click the AutoSum button, and Excel inserts the formulas that sum the rows and the columns.

	A	B	C	D	E	F
1		Sales Q1	Sales Q2	Sales Q3	Sales Q4	
2	East	30	30	40	10	
3	West	40	20	50	30	
4	North	40	10	30	20	
5	South	40	20	50	50	
6						
7						

- To create AutoSum formulas for only *some* values, select a range of contiguous cells and then click AutoSum. The selected range can span multiple rows or columns but can't be a noncontiguous range or a multiple selection.

	A	B	C	D	E	F
1		Sales Q1	Sales Q2	Sales Q3	Sales Q4	
2	East	30	30	40	10	
3	West	40	20	50	30	
4	North	40	10	30	20	
5	South	40	20	50	50	
6						

- If you haven't already formatted the cell targeted to hold the AutoSum formula, then AutoSum applies the same number format used by the first cell in the summed range.

- If your data are in a table (Insert tab > Tables group > Table), then AutoSum creates SUBTOTAL formulas at the bottom of the table instead of SUM formulas. If the table rows are filtered, then the SUBTOTAL function sums only the visible cells.

21

Summing Tricks

Advanced summing formulas let you sum cells that meet complex selection criteria. The sample workbook has worksheets that use the formulas in this chapter.

Calculating a Cumulative Sum

A **cumulative sum** (or **running total**) is a cell-by-cell calculation that uses progressively more values, starting with a single value (the first value), continuing with more values in the order in which they're listed, and ending with all the values.

The sample workbook has a worksheet that contains rainfall amounts for a 7-day period in cells B2:B8.

	C2			f_x	=SUM(B$2:B2)	
	A	B	C	D	E	F
1	day	rainfall	week-to-date			
2	Mon	0.5	0.5			
3	Tue	0	0.5			
4	Wed	1.5	2			
5	Thu	2.5	4.5			
6	Fri		4.5			
7	Sat		4.5			
8	Sun		4.5			
9	Total	4.5				

The formula in cell C2 is

=SUM(B$2:B2)

The dollar sign ($) in the B$2:B2 reference anchors the first cell (B$2) in the reference to the same row (here, row 2). When this formula is copied down the column, the range argument always starts with row 2 and ends with the current row. After copying this formula down column C, the formula in cell C5, for example, is

=SUM(B$2:B5)

Tip: The reference in the preceding formula is called a **mixed reference**, created by preceding either the column value or the row value with a dollar sign $ to "lock" either the column or the row. To switch quickly among mixed ($A1 or A$1), relative (A1), and absolute ($A$1) references, select the reference that you want to change (in the formula bar, highlight the reference or click anywhere in it), and then press F4 to cycle through reference types.

To hide cumulative sums for rows with no values, use the IF function to test for blank cells. Copy the following formula from cell C2 down the column:

=IF(B2<>"",SUM(B$2:B2),"")

	A	B	C	D	E	F
1	day	rainfall	week-to-date			
2	Mon	0.5	0.5			
3	Tue	0	0.5			
4	Wed	1.5	2			
5	Thu	2.5	4.5			
6	Fri					
7	Sat					
8	Sun					
9	Total	4.5				

Summing Extreme Values

To sum the n largest values in the range named *sum_extreme*, use the single-cell array formula:

`{=SUM(LARGE(sum_extreme,ROW(INDIRECT("1:`n`"))))}`

where n is a positive integer.

Similarly, the formula for summing the n smallest values is:

`{=SUM(SMALL(sum_extreme,ROW(INDIRECT("1:`n`"))))}`

To sum the top 10 values, for example, type:

`{=SUM(LARGE(sum_extreme,ROW(INDIRECT("1:10"))))}`

To sum the bottom 5 values, type:

`{=SUM(SMALL(sum_extreme,ROW(INDIRECT("1:5"))))}`

	A	B	C	D	E	F	G
1	48			676	Sum top 10 values		
2	83			102	Sum bottom 5 values		
3	53						
4	45			676	Sum top 10 values (array constant)		
5	88			102	Sum bottom 5 values (array constant)		
6	82						
7	55						
8	33						
9	40						
10	52						
11	17						
12	7						
13	66						
14	80						
15	13						
16	32						
17	52						
18	39						
19	53						
20	64						
21							

If n is small (say, $n \leq 10$), then it might be easier to type an array constant instead of a ROW expression. The single-cell array formula for the 10 largest values is:

    {=SUM(LARGE(sum_extreme,{1,2,3,4,5,6,7,8,9,10}))}

For the 5 smallest values, the formula is:

    {=SUM(SMALL(sum_extreme,{1,2,3,4,5}))}

Tip: If your data are in a table (Insert tab > Tables group > Table), then you can use autofiltering to hide all but the top n rows, and then sum them.

Summing Currency Amounts

Many types of financial formulas (such as loan calculations or percentage discounts or markups) can lead to rounding errors when summing currency amounts. Even "off-by-a-cent" values can accumulate to large errors when many such values are totaled. You can eliminate rounding errors by using the ROUND function. The following array formula, for example, rounds each currency amount in the range C2:C4 to two decimal places before summing them:

    {=SUM(ROUND(C2:C4,2))}

	A	B	C	D
1	price	discount	new price	
2	$10.00	13.50%	$8.65	
3	$5.00	10.35%	$4.48	
4	$1.00	5.55%	$0.94	
5			$14.08	Sum (unrounded)
6			$14.07	Sum (rounded)
7				

Keep in mind that the actual currency values have additional decimal places that are hidden by the number format. In this example, the unrounded value in cell C5 is actually $14.077, which displays as $14.08.

You can also eliminate rounding errors by using ROUND in the formula that calculates each row total (which doesn't need an array formula).

Summing Every Nth Value in a Range

Summing every nth value in a range is useful for calculations involving periodic or statistical samples. The following array formula sums every nth value in the range named *sum_n*, where n is an integer ≥ 0 and *sum_n* is a single-column (vertical) range:

```
{=IF(n=0,0,SUM(IF(MOD(ROW(INDIRECT("1:"&
COUNT(sum_n)))-1,n)=0,sum_n,"")))}
```

The preceding formula sums the first cell, the $(n + 1)$th cell, the $(2n + 1)$th cell, and so on until the end of the range *sum_n*. If cell C1 contains the value 2, for example, then the following array formula sums every second cell in *sum_n*:

```
{=IF(C1=0,0,SUM(IF(MOD(ROW(INDIRECT("1:"&
COUNT(sum_n)))-1,C1)=0,sum_n,"")))}
```

	A	B	C	D	E
1	1			2	n
2	2			100	Sum of every nth value
3	3				
4	4				
5	5				
6	6				
7	7				
8	8				
9	9				
10	10				
11	11				
12	12				
13	13				
14	14				
15	15				
16	16				
17	17				
18	18				
19	19				
20	20				

This array formula works by creating an internal array of consecutive integers {1, 2, 3,...}, which the MOD function transforms into an array of the remainders when each row number is divided by n. If an element in this array is 0 (that is, evenly divisible by n), then the corresponding cell in the range *sum_n* is included in the sum. The outer IF function handles the special case where $n = 0$ (the sum of no values).

You can use the TRANSPOSE function to make the array formula work with a single-row (horizontal) range:

```
{=IF(n=0,0,SUM(IF(MOD(TRANSPOSE(ROW(INDIRECT("1:"&
COUNT(sum_n))))-1,n)=0,sum_n,"")))}
```

Summing Values Based on a Single Criterion (SUMIF)

The SUMIF function adds values in a range that meet a single criterion:

SUMIF(*range, criteria,* [*sum_range*])

where

range (required) is the range of cells containing values to evaluate by using *criteria* to determine which cells are summed.

criteria (required) is a number, expression, cell reference, text string, or function that determines which cells will be summed. For example, *criteria* can be expressed as 25, "25", ">25", "widgets", B4, or TODAY(). Any text criteria or any criteria that include logical or mathematical symbols must be enclosed in double quotes ("). If *criteria* is numeric, then double quotes aren't required. You can use the wildcard characters, question mark (?) and asterisk (*), in *criteria*. A question mark matches any single character; an asterisk matches any sequence of characters. To find an actual question mark or asterisk, type a tilde (~) before the character.

sum_range (optional) is the range that contains the actual cells to sum, if you want to sum cells other than those specified in *range*. If *sum_range* is omitted, then SUMIF sums the cells in *range* (that is, the same cells to which *criteria* is applied).

Tip: If *sum_range* and *range* aren't the same size, then the actual cells summed are determined by using the top-left cell in *sum_range* as the beginning cell, and then including cells that correspond in size and shape of *range*. If *range* is A1:A5 and *sum_range* is B1:B3, for example, then the actual cells added are B1:B5. If *range* is A1:B4 and *sum_range* is C1:C2, then the actual cells added are C1:D4. If *range* and *sum_range* are unequal in size, then the recalculation time of SUMIF increases.

	A	B	C	D
1	account	type	opened	balance
2	A111	savings	5	400
3	A111	checking	10	200
4	A222	savings	20	100
5	A333	checking	5	300
6	A444	savings	5	0
7	A444	checking	10	-500
8	A555	savings	0	-400
9	A777	savings	5	400
10	A888	savings	10	-200
11	A888	checking	10	100
12				
13		200	Sum balances = 100	
14		200	Sum balances = 100 (array formula)	
15		1300	Sum balances > 100	
16		1300	Sum balances > 100 (array formula)	
17		-1100	Sum negative balances	
18		-1100	Sum negative balances (array formula)	
19		400	Sum balances <> 0	
20		400	Sum balances <> 0 (array formula)	
21		700	Sum balances where opened < 10	
22		700	Sum balances where opened < 10 (array formula)	
23		100	Sum balances where type = checking (case-insensitive)	
24		100	Sum balances where type = checking (array formula, case-insensitive)	
25		-200	Sum balances where account <> A111 (case-insensitive)	
26		-200	Sum balances where account <> A111 (array formula, case-insensitive)	

The following examples show several ways to use SUMIF in formulas. The *criteria* argument in the examples is hardcoded in the SUMIF function, but *criteria* can also be a range name or cell address that contains the criteria (=SUMIF(range,B4), for example, where cell B4 contains the value <>0.).

=SUMIF(range,10)

Sums cells in *range* containing the value 10. The equivalent array formula is {=SUM(IF(range=10,range))}.

=SUMIF(range,">10")
: Sums cells in *range* greater than 10. The equivalent array formula is {=SUM(IF(range>10,range))}.

=SUMIF(range,"<0")
: Sums cells in *range* containing a negative value. The equivalent array formula is {=SUM(IF(range<0,range))}.

=SUMIF(range,"<>0")
: Sums cells in *range* not equal to 0. The equivalent array formula is {=SUM(IF(range<>0,range))}.

=SUMIF(range,"<0",sum_range)
: Sums cells in *sum_range* where the corresponding cells in *range* are negative. The equivalent array formula is {=SUM(IF(range<0,sum_range))}.

=SUMIF(range2,"=string",sum_range)
: Sums cells in *sum_range* where the corresponding cells in *range2* are "string" (case-insensitive). The equivalent array formula is {=SUM(IF(range2="string",sum_range))}.

Tip: When testing for equality, the equal sign is optional: the equivalent SUMIF formula is =SUMIF(range2,"string",sum_range).

=SUMIF(range2,"<>string",sum_range)
: Sums cells in *sum_range* where the corresponding cells in *range2* are not "string" (case-insensitive). The equivalent array formula is {=SUM(IF(range2<>"string",sum_range))}.

=SUMIF(range3,">="&DATE(2013,6,1),sum_range)
: Sums cells in *sum_range* where the corresponding cells in *range3* contain dates falling on or after 1-June-2013. The second argument is an expression that uses a quote-enclosed comparison operator (">=") concatenated (using the & operator) with the result of the DATE function, which returns the specified date as a serial number.

The equivalent array formula is {=SUM(IF(range3>=DATE(2013, 6,1),sum_range))}.

=SUMIF(range3,">="&TODAY(),sum_range)
Sums cells in *sum_range* where the corresponding cells in *range3* contain dates falling on or after today's date. The equivalent array formula is {=SUM(IF(range3>=TODAY(),sum_range))}.

Tip: For more ways to specify criteria, see "Counting Cells Based on a Single Criterion (COUNTIF)" on page 113.

Summing Values Based on Multiple Criteria (SUMIFS)

The SUMIFS function adds values in a range that meet multiple criteria:

SUMIFS(*sum_range, criteria_range1, criteria1, [criteria_range2, criteria2],...*)

where

sum_range (required) is the range that contains the cells to sum, including numbers or names, arrays, ranges, or cell references that contain numbers. Blank and text values are ignored.

Tip: Note that *sum_range* is the first argument in SUMIFS but the third argument in SUMIF. If you're copying and pasting between these two functions, then be sure to reorder the arguments.

criteria_range1 (required) is the first range of cells in which to evaluate the associated criteria.

criteria1 (required) is a number, expression, cell reference, text string, or function that determines which cells will be summed. For example, *criteria* can be expressed as 25, "25", ">25", "widgets", B4, or TODAY(). Any text criteria or any criteria that include logical or mathematical symbols must be enclosed in double quotes ("). You can use the wildcard characters, question mark (?) and asterisk (*), in *criteria*. A question mark matches any single character; an asterisk matches any sequence of characters. To find an actual question mark or asterisk, type a tilde (~) before the character.

criteria_range2, criteria2,... (optional) are additional ranges and their associated criteria. Each *criteria_range* argument must contain the same number of rows and columns as *sum_range*. The ranges don't have to be adjacent to each other. Up to 127 range–criteria pairs are allowed.

Tip: SUMIFS is available in Excel 2007 or later.

	A	B	C	D
1	account	type	opened	balance
2	A111	savings	5	400
3	A111	checking	10	200
4	A222	savings	20	100
5	A333	checking	5	300
6	A444	savings	5	0
7	A444	checking	10	-500
8	A555	savings	0	-400
9	A777	savings	5	400
10	A888	savings	10	-200
11	A888	checking	10	100
12				
28	Using AND Logic for Sums			
29		200 Sum balance for type = savings and opened <= 10 (SUMIFS; Excel 2007 or later)		
30		200 Sum balance for type = savings and opened <= 10 (array formula)		
31		200 Sum balance for type = savings and opened <= 10 (SUMPRODUCT)		
32				
33	Using OR Logic for Sums			
34		500 Sum balance for type = checking or opened <= 5 (array formula)		
35				
36	Mixing AND and OR Logic for Sums			
37		100 Sum balance opened >= 10 and account is A111 or A888 (SUMIFS; Excel 2007 or later)		
38		100 Sum balance opened >= 10 and account is A111 or A888 (array formula)		

Using AND Logic for Sums

Use AND logic in formulas to sum cells that meet *all* specified criteria. For example, to sums cells in the range named *balance* that meet the criteria

$$(\text{type is savings}) \text{ AND } (\text{opened} <= 10)$$

use the following formula:

148   Pay Off Your Mortgage Early With Excel!

```
=SUMIFS(balance,type,"savings",opened,"<=10")
```

In Excel 2003 or earlier, use the following equivalent array formula:

```
{=SUM((type="savings")*(opened<=10)*balance)}
```

The preceding array formula creates two internal logical (TRUE/FALSE) arrays. Each element in the first array is TRUE if the corresponding *type* value equals "savings"; otherwise, it's FALSE. Each element in the second array is TRUE if the corresponding *opened* value is less than or equal to 10; otherwise, it's FALSE. Multiplying logical values yields TRUE × TRUE = 1; TRUE × FALSE = 0; and FALSE × FALSE = 0. Each corresponding *balance* value is nonzero only if the corresponding values in the two logical arrays are both TRUE.

To use an equivalent SUMPRODUCT formula, multiply the logical arguments by 1 to convert each TRUE value to 1 and each FALSE value to 0:

```
=SUMPRODUCT(1*(type="savings"),1*(opened<=10),
balance)
```

See also "Using AND Logic for Counts" on page 116.

Using OR Logic for Sums

Use OR logic in formulas to sum cells that meet *any* specified criteria. For example, to sums cells in the range named *balance* that meet the criteria

(type is checking) OR (opened <= 5)

use the following array formula:

```
{=SUM(IF((type="checking")+(opened<=5),1,0)*
balance)}
```

To insert more OR conditions, add more plus-sign (+) expressions to the formula.

See also "Using OR Logic for Counts" on page 118.

Mixing AND and OR Logic for Sums

Summing multiple SUMIFS functions lets you combine AND and OR logic in a single formula. For example, to sum cells that meet the criteria (opened >= 10) AND ((account is A111) OR (account is A888))

use the following formula:

```
=SUMIFS(balance,opened,">=10",account,"A111")+
SUMIFS(balance,opened,">=10",account,"A888")
```

The preceding formula requires repeating the AND criteria in every SUMIFS function, which is unwieldy for formulas that involve many criteria. A more-concise array formula (also for use in Excel 2003 or earlier) is:

```
{=SUM((opened>=10)*IF((account="A111")+
(account="A888"),1)*balance)}
```

See also "Mixing AND and OR Logic for Counts" on page 119.

Index

Symbols

1904 date system 60
(cell display) 59, 63, 96
#N/A error 111, 119, 136
#NUM! error 6, 25, 34

A

amortization 41
amortization schedules 41–48
Analysis ToolPak 129
annual percentage rate (APR) 38
annuities 14, 16
arithmetic rounding 9
array formulas 3
AutoSum 136

B

banker's rounding 10

C

calculation, controlling in Excel 49
cash flows 5
circular references 4
COLUMNS function 107, 109
compound interest 20, 37
converting interest rates 37–39
COUNTA function 107, 110
COUNTBLANK function 107, 109
COUNT function 107, 110
COUNTIF function 107, 112, 113
COUNTIFS function 108, 115
counts. *See also* sums
   calculating without formulas 104
   calculations with 107–112, 113–124
   frequency distributions 125–132
   functions 107
   mode 119
   of text strings 122
   of unique values 121
   sample workbook 102
credit-card payoffs 32
CUMIPMT function 35
CUMPRINC function 35

D

data tables 49–54
DATEDIF function 83
DATE function 72
dates. *See* dates and times
dates and times
   1904 date system 60
   arithmetic 85, 95
   calculations with dates 85–93
   calculations with times 95–99
   combining 66
   converting from text 88, 98
   day-month-year order 62
   days vs. nights 60
   entering
      dates 57, 60, 72
      times 57, 65, 72

formatting
  autoformatting 68
  dates 57, 62, 67
  default 61
  times 57, 65, 67, 95
  functions 71–84
  generating series of 86, 97
  January 0, 1900 59, 66
  leap years 68, 89
  precision of times 64
  problem dates 68
  Roman numerals 88
  sample workbook 55
  searching for dates 63
  serial numbers 59, 63
  static values (literals) 72
  two-digit years 69
  valid ranges 59, 66, 69
  vs. text 70
DATEVALUE function 77
DAY function 75
DAYS360 function 78
DCOUNTA function 108
DCOUNT function 108
DSUM function 133

E

EDATE function 79
EFFECT function 38
effective interest rate 38
EOMONTH function 81
Excel
  accuracy of financial functions 9
  Analysis ToolPak 129
  array formulas 3
  AutoSum 136
  calculation, controlling 49
  circular references 4
  conditional formatting 47
  data tables 49–54
  errors
    ###### 59, 63, 96
    #N/A 111, 119, 136
    #NUM! 6, 25, 34
  Goal Seek 8
  iteration 25

keyboard shortcuts 10, 57, 68
named ranges 2
percentages, entering 7
pivot tables 105, 132
rounding numbers 9–12, 142
sample workbook 2, 55, 102
status bar 104
tables 104

F

fixed income 30
formatting numbers 7, 10
formulas
  array formulas 3
  circular references 4
  named ranges 2
frequency distributions 125–132
FREQUENCY function 108, 125
functions
  accuracy of financial 9
  counting 107
  date and time 71
  financial 6
  rounding 9
  summing 133
  using in formulas 2
future value 8
  FV function 19–22
  of a lump sum 21
  of payments 20
  of payments and a lump sum 22
fv argument 8
FV function 19–22
  arguments of 7

G

Goal Seek 8
guess argument 8, 25

H

HOUR function 76

I

interest rates
  annual percentage rate (APR) 38
  compound 20, 37

converting 37–39
effective 38
growth rates 26
nominal 37
of interest-free loans 27
of retirement accounts 26
of short-term (payday) loans 26
periodic 38
picking 13
RATE function 25–27
time periods of 5
types of quotes 37
IPMT function 33
ISLOGICAL function 111
ISNONTEXT function 111
ISTEXT function 111
iteration 25

L

leap years 68, 89
loans
  amortization 41
  amortization schedules 41–48
  automobile 24
  cash flows 5
  comparing 49–54
  credit-card payoff 32
  early payoff 31
  interest-free 27
  principal and interest payments 33–35
  short-term (payday) 26
lump sums 15, 16, 21, 22

M

Microsoft Excel. *See* Excel
MINUTE function 76
MODE function 119
MONTH function 75
mortgages. *See* loans

N

named ranges 2
NETWORKDAYS function 82
NOMINAL function 38
nominal interest rate 37

NOW function 71
nper argument 7
NPER function 29–32
  arguments of 7

P

payday loans 26
payments
  amortization schedules 41–48
  as cash flows 5
  comparing loans 49–54
  date of first 5
  days vs. nights 5
  deferred-start 17
  down payments 5
  fixed income 30
  in advance 5
  in arrears 5
  interest portion of 33–35
  loan 24
  PMT function 23–24
  principal portion of 33–35
  retirement 24, 30
  time periods of 5
  type argument 8
  variable 17
  vs. receipts 5
percentages, entering in Excel 7
periodic interest rate 38
pivot tables 105, 132
pmt argument 8
PMT function 23–24
  accuracy of 9
  arguments of 7
PPMT function 33
present value 8
  of a lump sum 15
  of an annuity 14
  of an annuity with a lump sum 16
  of deferred-start payments 17
  of variable payments 17
  PV function 13–18
pv argument 8
PV function 13–18
  arguments of 7

R

rate argument 7
RATE function 25-27
  arguments of 7
receipts 5
rounding numbers 9-12
  arithmetic rounding 9
  banker's rounding 10
  examples 10
  summing rounded numbers 142
rounding times 99
ROWS function 108, 109

S

sample workbook 2, 55, 102
SECOND function 76
serial numbers, dates and times 59, 63
SUBTOTAL function 108, 133, 138
SUM function 133, 134
SUMIF function 133, 144
SUMIFS function 133, 147
SUMPRODUCT function 134, 149
sums. *See also* counts
  AutoSum 136
  calculating without formulas 104
  calculations with 133-138, 139-150
  cumulative (running) 139
  functions 133
  ignoring error values 136
  of every n-th value 143
  of extreme values 141
  of rounded numbers 142
  sample workbook 102

T

TIME function 72
times. *See* dates and times
TIMEVALUE function 77
time value of money 4
TODAY function 71
type argument 8

W

WEEKDAY function 78
WEEKNUM function 83
WORKDAY function 82

Y

YEARFRAC function 80
YEAR function 75

www.ingramcontent.com/pod-product-compliance
Lightning Source LLC
Chambersburg PA
CBHW070639220526
45466CB00001B/234